hand knits for the home

Published in 2004 by Conran Octopus Limited
a part of the Octopus Publishing Group
2–4 Heron Quays, London E14 4JP
Visit our website at www.conran-octopus.co.uk

British Library Cataloguing-in-Publication Data. A catalogue record
for this book is available from the British Library.

Publishing Director: Lorraine Dickey
Art Director: Chi Lam
Art Editor: Carl Hodson
Executive Editor: Zia Mattocks
Editors: Emma Clegg and Libby Willis
Photographer: Damian Russell
Stylist: Melinda Ashton Turner
Illustrator: Russell Bell
Production Manager: Angela Couchman

ISBN 1 84091 345 2

Printed in China

hand knits for the home

Over 20 specially commissioned projects for stylish interiors

Caroline Birkett

photography by Damian Russell styling by Melinda Ashton Turner

It is incredibly satisfying to make something for your home with only a ball of wool and two needles. Constructing new and exciting fabrics by combining different yarns and stitches makes knitting creative and rewarding, even at the most basic level. When you start knitting, I would advise choosing chunky yarns knitted in the simplest of stitches on big needles, and then you will soon be sinking back into a pile of sumptuous hand-knitted cushions.

Tracking the origins of knitting is hampered by the fact that textiles deteriorate severely over time, making early fragments very rare. Some sources say that early samples from Egypt and the Middle East are the first-known evidence of the craft. It is likely that knitting developed from an early sewing or crochet-type technique, possibly in more than one geographical location. Arabic pieces from the seventh century AD were already using sophisticated stranded colourwork, but it was some time later that textured knits were developed. Because of the inherent elasticity of knitted fabric, the development of the craft largely relates to its use as a form of clothing. Discoveries in Spain dated to the thirteenth century AD, however, record two surprisingly modern-looking cushions covered with a heraldic-style pattern in two-colour Fair Isle, one with tassels at each corner.

Knitting is a soothing pastime: research actually suggests that it offers a therapeutic antidote to our hectic lives. The repetition and rhythm of the knitting movement has been shown to have a calming effect, leading to a decrease in heart rate, blood pressure and muscle tension.

As well as an overview of techniques, projects are included for knitted cushion covers, throws, blankets, mats, bags and runners. These vary in complexity, some using basic knit-and-purl structures and others more advanced techniques such as intarsia and beading. I just hope that you will enjoy the process of knitting as much as your final creations. The textural character and the yielding nature of knitted soft furnishings certainly make them the ultimate in interior style and comfort.

Getting Started

Knitting tools and accessories

One of the joys of knitting is that relatively little equipment is needed, even at advanced levels, and what is required is inexpensive and portable. The only real essentials are knitting needles and yarn, plus a sewing needle to attach any pieces together at the end of the process. There are, however, a number of other items that will make life easier and help to achieve a better finish.

Standard needles – sometimes called pins, these are used in pairs to produce a flat knitted fabric. Occasionally you may want to use three needles to produce a very wide flat piece, such as a throw. Each needle has a closed end and a tip tapering to a rounded point. The tip is used to form the stitches while the long, cylindrical section holds the stitches after they have been worked and sets the stitch size. Needles must be strong, light, smooth and durable. I prefer bamboo needles, as they are pleasant to handle, warm and light in weight, but needles are also made of aluminium, plastic or wood. All these materials are suitable, as they have a smooth surface on which stitches slide easily, making knitting faster. However, do take care because on a highly polished surface there is also an increased risk of dropping stitches, particularly when working with a silky yarn. Very thick needles tend to be made only in plastic, to minimize their weight. Look after your needles, as a rough surface or a tip that is too blunt will make knitting difficult and slow. Needles come in a range of sizes from 2mm (no 14/US 0) to 15mm (US 19) and vary in length between 25cm (10in) and 40cm (16in). The choice of needle thickness depends on the weight of the yarn to be knitted and how tightly you knit. The choice

of needle length will depend on the way that you hold your needles and the width of the item to be knitted.

There are also needles that have rounded points at both ends, called double-pointed needles, but these are used for advanced techniques such as tubular knitting and knitting medallions, which are not covered here.

Cable needles – these taper to a rounded point at both ends but are shorter than double-pointed needles at about 13cm (5in) long. They are used to hold stitches during the crossover in cabling and some have a v-shaped kink to prevent the stitches from accidentally falling off. They are sized in the same way as standard needles.

Circular needles or **twinpins** – these have rigid ends joined by a length of strong, flexible plastic cord. They are used for knitting large, flat items such as throws and for tubular knitting. Their thickness is sized in the same way as standard needles, and tip to tip they vary in length between 40cm (16in) and 120cm (47¼in).

Sewing needle – this is needed when constructing a finished item to stitch together pieces that have been knitted separately and

to darn in ends of yarn. It must have a large eye to allow the sewing yarn to pass through without being damaged and a blunt point that will pass between the knitted stitches easily to avoid splitting the yarn within the fabric. Keep a selection of needles in different sizes for use with different weights of yarn: wool needles for bulky yarns and tapestry needles for finer yarns.

Tape measure or **ruler** – this is essential when establishing the correct tension (gauge) for your work to measure the area over which to count the required number of stitches. During knitting and when blocking finished pieces, you will also need to check the length and width of knitted pieces against the measurements in the pattern. Work consistently in either centimetres or inches because the two are not interchangeable.

Wool pins – these are used for pinning seams, blocking and marking tension swatches. The 5cm (2in) chrome, glass-headed pins you can buy are easy to see in knitting and their large head anchors well in more open knits.

Scissors – a sharp, medium-sized pair of scissors will be needed for trimming ends and cutting yarn. Never attempt to snap a yarn, as it may stretch or even rob yarn from the knitted piece of work, making the stitches uneven in size.

Bobbins – these are useful when a number of different yarns are being used simultaneously to prevent them becoming tangled. You can make simple homemade bobbins from squares of card with a slit cut in or buy plastic purpose-made ones. Wind a length of yarn around the bobbin, then, as you work, unwind short lengths and secure in the slit each time to prevent further unravelling.

Crochet hook – this is useful for picking up dropped stitches and making fringes. It can also be used in place of the right-hand needle to cast off (bind off) with.

Row counter – this is a small plastic cylinder that fits on the end of the knitting needle. Turning the top on the completion of each row operates a small number counter.

Needle gauge – this is a piece of plastic or metal with holes that correspond to the standard needle sizes. To check the size of a needle, find the hole into which it fits most snugly. This is particularly useful for circular and cable needles, as once they are separated from their packaging there is nothing to indicate their size.

Stitch stopper – placed on the end of the knitting needle when the piece is not being worked, this will stop the stitches slipping off. A wine-bottle cork does the same job.

Knitting yarns

Hand knitting is a very tactile craft. If you choose a yarn that you enjoy knitting with, you will probably enjoy using the finished article. When you are looking at yarn, think about more than just its appearance. Touch it and imagine how it might feel when it is knitted into a cushion or throw. A yarn such as cotton, with a cool, dry handle and smooth surface, is ideal for summer soft furnishings, whereas a warmer and more textured yarn such as mohair would make a wonderful throw to snuggle up in on a winter's evening.

If you have a particular pattern in mind, it is easiest, at first, to use the yarn specified, although yarns with an identical recommended number of stitches and rows over a given area can be used. Also look for a yarn with a similar length to a given weight, or the feel of the fabric and yarn quantity requirements could be affected. Think carefully before substituting another yarn because, for example, if the pattern is a knit and purl texture, that beautiful bouclé yarn will not really be suitable, as it will mask the pattern, hiding all your hard work.

Heavier yarns are easier to knit than finer ones because the loops are very visible and your work will grow much more quickly. Some yarns, such as hairy or bouclé ones, are a little more difficult to knit with than others but will also mask any variation in stitch size, and because of their fullness they knit up more quickly than you might expect. So do not be put off these types of yarn if they create the look you want.

Yarn is made by twisting fibres together to give them strength and to form a continuous, usable length. The character of a yarn is determined by the types of fibres used, the way in which they are spun and any finishing process that is applied.

Types of fibre

The fibres in a yarn can come from natural or manmade sources. Sheep wool, alpaca and cashmere are hairs from animal coats; cotton and linen fibres are derived from plants; and some manmade yarns are made from mineral sources such as oil. Each type of fibre looks, feels and acts differently. Most can be used alone or mixed with other fibres to create a particular appearance or produce a blend of properties. Knowing about these characteristics will help you to choose the right type of yarn.

Wool

Although technically all animal hair can be categorized as wool, what most people think of as wool is the fleece of the sheep. This is by far the most widely used type of yarn for knitting, and is available in a diverse choice of weights and colours. Knitted fabrics that are made from woollen yarns can be fluffy, cosy and comfortable or sleek, smooth and shiny, depending on the age and breed of sheep that the fleece comes from and exactly how the fibres were spun. Lambswool, for example, uses the first shearing of young sheep and is therefore significantly softer than subsequent shearings. At the other end of the scale, the fleece of the Shetland sheep is of a much coarser grade than the fine wool of the Spanish merino sheep – this is because it comes from a hardy mountain breed that lives in a much more inhospitable climate.

The fibres can be combed so that only the longer ones remain, lying parallel to each other, to form a smooth yarn. If a mix of fibre lengths are used and left uncombed, this results in a hairier, more rustic yarn. Yarns spun from wool are generally easy to knit with because they have a natural elasticity and good resilience, forming stitches that are even in shape and size. This makes woollen yarns a good choice for those who are new to the craft. Take care when washing woollen fabrics, as they can felt, which is an irreversible process whereby the fibres matt together and the piece shrinks. This process can be used in a controlled way to create a dense, inelastic fabric but it can also easily ruin a very valued piece.

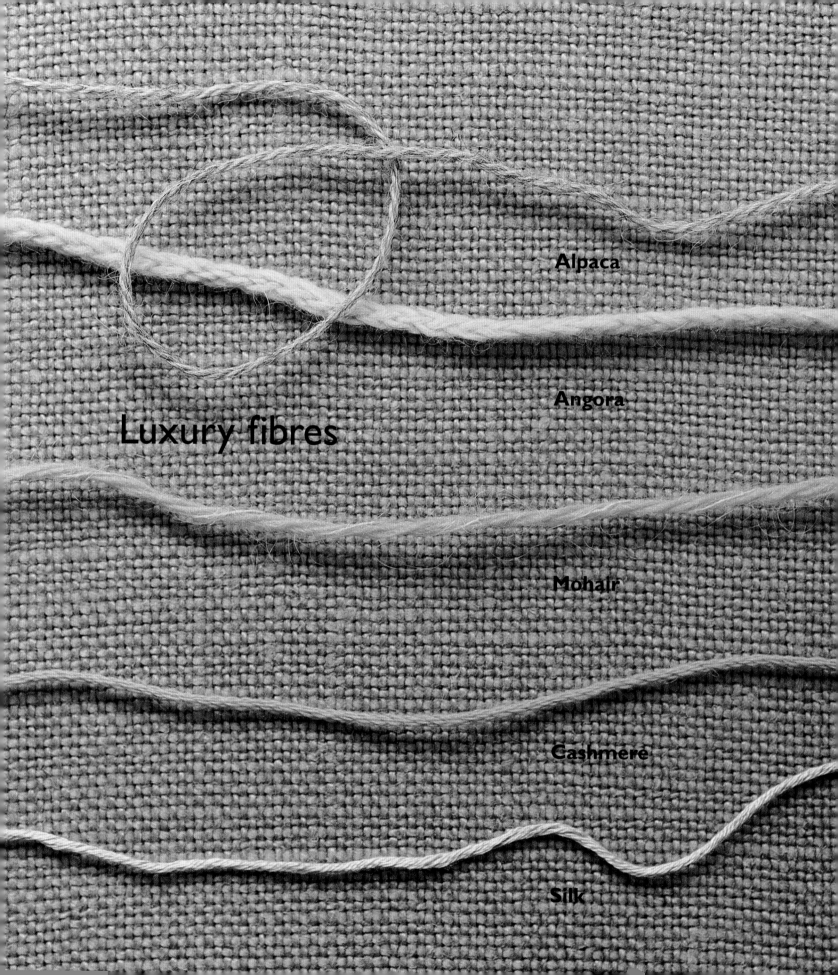

Luxury fibres

Alpaca

Angora

Mohair

Cashmere

Silk

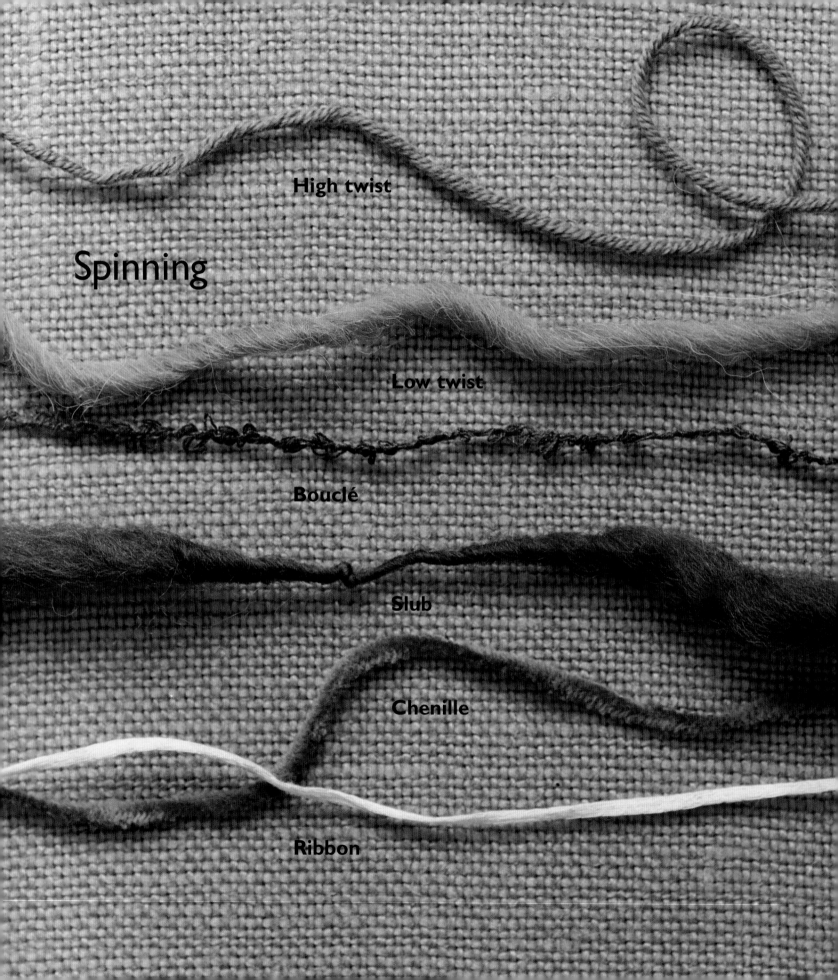

High twist

Spinning

Low twist

Bouclé

Slub

Chenille

Ribbon

Cotton and linen

Cotton is a natural plant fibre that grows in the seedcase of the cotton bush after the blossom has fallen. Cotton fabrics tend to have a smooth surface with a clear definition that shows any textured stitches well. They are dry and soft to the touch and hang in a heavy, relaxed way as cotton is much less elastic than wool. This lack of elasticity means that cotton can be a little more difficult to knit with, but the fabrics tend to lie flatter.

Linen is made from the woody fibre taken from the stem of the flax plant and put through a very complex series of processes to produce a finished yarn. Linen yarns have little or no elasticity, which makes them impractical for knitting unless they are blended with other fibres. Linen can add a lustrous sheen, a stiff handle and sophisticated natural colour to a blend and is often mixed with cotton or silk.

Luxury fibres

Alpaca fibres come from the alpaca, an animal belonging to the llama family. It has a long, slightly curly coat, which produces a soft and lustrous yarn. It is available in a beautiful range of natural as well as dyed colours.

Angora fibres are combed from the coat of the angora rabbit. The delicate hairs are white and silky, fine and slippery. They are usually spun with another fibre such as lambswool because they are difficult to spin alone. Angora yarn is best knitted loosely to allow space for its fluffy character to come out.

Mohair comes from the angora goat and the long hairs are usually spun with some wool and nylon to enhance their strength. Yarn can be brushed or unbrushed and fabrics can also be brushed when knitted up, to raise the hairs. The hairy appearance can be deceptive, for even when it is spun to a fine core, mohair can be knitted to the same tension as a much thicker yarn. Mohair fabrics are light and airy but also quite stable because the hairs hold them in shape. Kid mohair, from young goats, is the best quality.

Cashmere is combed, not shorn, from the undercoat of the cashmere goat and spun into the ultimate luxury yarn, ultra-soft to the touch and with a subtly lustrous appearance. Yarn of 100 per cent cashmere is extremely expensive because each goat produces only a small amount of fibre each year, hence blends with silk or extra-fine merino wool are common.

Silk is produced by certain types of silkworm to make their cocoons. It is very strong so it can be spun to make extremely fine yarns. Depending on how the fibres are processed, silk can vary from smooth, sleek yarns, which make fluid, elegant fabrics, to silk noiles, which are rough and dry to the touch.

Synthetics

Made with chemicals, synthetic fibres lack the character of natural fibres, but they are cheap, strong and durable. Because of this they are often used in blends with natural fibres and are also useful in some of the more elaborate spinning techniques.

Other materials

All kinds of things can be used to knit with, including ribbon, string, raffia, plastic bags, cotton and wool rags, suede – in fact, any flexible material that can be made into a usable, continuous length.

Yarn construction

Most plain yarns are made up from a number of strands called ply; these are twisted individually, then twisted together for strength.

4-ply yarns are the finest yarns commonly in use. They are knitted on needles of around 3mm (no 11/US 3) to about 28–30 stitches per 10cm (4in) of stocking- (stockinette-) stitch fabric.

Double-knitting yarns are versatile and used to knit a wide variety of fabrics from cables to openwork. It is usually almost double the thickness of 4-ply yarn and knitted on needles of around 4mm (no 8/US 6) to about 22–24 stitches per 10cm (4in) of stocking-stitch fabric.

Aran yarns are traditionally used to knit heavy textured and cabled designs. They are knitted on needles of around 5mm (no 6/US 8) to about 18 stitches per 10cm (4in) of stocking-stitch fabric.

Chunky and double-double knitting are extra-thick yarns which are knitted on needles of around 7mm (no 2/US 10½) to about 13 stitches per 10cm (4in) of stocking-stitch fabric.

These are only guidelines, as the thickness of yarns in each category will vary. Not all double-knitting yarns are the same thickness and consequently may require a different tension. This is significant when you wish to substitute a different type of yarn and the finished size of the fabric is important. You must then knit a tension swatch to check suitability (see pages 24–5).

Spinning

In addition to the character of the fibres, yarns can also be given a distinct texture and handle in spinning. Twist gives cohesion to the fibres, and the more twist, the stronger the yarn. High-twist yarns tend to be crisp and firm. They knit into fabrics where the stitches are clearly defined and they tend to drape well. Yarns with a low level of twist are soft and full but weaker. Soft yarns fill the spaces between the stitches and rows to create a dense, inflexible fabric.

Classic, smooth yarns, spun to a regular thickness, show stitch patterns beautifully, while fancy yarns are constructed to have a strongly characteristic appearance and are better used with simpler stitches.

Bouclé is a looped yarn built around a thin but strong supporting thread. Bouclé fabrics are light and airy and their looped texture shows best on purl stitches.

Slub yarn has areas along its length that are loosely twisted and thicker than others, lending the fabric a homespun, uneven character.

Chenille is a velvety yarn with pile, usually cotton, spun around a core. It is knitted on a small needle to create a dense, even fabric with a sumptuous, full handle. Once knitted it can be hard to unravel without damaging the pile.

Ribbon yarn is woven or knitted, not twisted, making it flat, whereas most yarns are round in cross-section. This creates a depth in fabrics using purl stitch and an almost spongy handle.

Yarn is supplied in balls or hanks, most commonly 25g (⅞oz), 50g (1¾oz) or 100g (3½oz), and on cones of greater weights. Balls usually have a ball band with information about the yarn weight, composition and washing instructions. Heavier yarns such as Aran and chunky are usually supplied in hanks or on cones. Yarn can be used directly from a ball or cone but hanks must first be wound by hand into balls. Wrap the yarn over your fingers then slip them out, leaving the yarn loosely wrapped (otherwise the yarn will be stretched while in the ball and after knitting it could relax, making the stitches smaller than they were and the tension or gauge too tight). Because yarns vary in thickness, balls of the same weight may be very different sizes and contain different lengths of yarn. A 50g (1¾oz) ball of a thick yarn will be shorter in length than a finer one, but fewer balls will be needed to knit a piece of fabric of the same size.

Colour

Some fibres, particularly animal hairs, are naturally coloured in a wonderful range of browns, beiges, greys and creams that can be used undyed. To achieve the full spectrum of colours, yarn can be dyed either before or after it is spun. Yarn dyed to a dark colour can be thinner and heavier than the same yarn in a lighter colour, leading to a looser and more open appearance when knitted to the same tension.

Heather mix, sometimes also called melange yarn, has fibres of different colours mixed together within the ply, which creates a subtle, tweedy look. Different fibres take dye differently, so within a blended yarn some fibres may be darker than others even when they were dyed the same colour.

Colour-twist or **marl** yarn has strands or plies of different colours that are twisted together to make a flecked mix where the colours are more separate.

Space-dyed yarn has sections along its length that are dyed to different colours, or different colour tones. It knits into fabric with a random mix of colours without the need to change yarns.

Knops or small bobbles of fibre can be added to yarn for extra colour and texture.

Yarn is dyed in batches called dye lots and the number of the dye lot should be marked somewhere on the ball band or cone label. The colour can vary very slightly between dye lots so try not to mix them, especially within areas of plain colour where any difference would be most noticeable.

Natural

Colour

Heather mix

Marl

Space-dyed

Knops

Casting on

Casting on puts the first row of loops on the needle. This creates the foundation upon which all the subsequent stitches are built, so the loops need to be even in size and spacing. The cast-on and cast-off also form two of the edges of a piece of work, so they need to have some give but also be durable and keep the whole piece in shape. The edges are particularly important if they are not to be incorporated in a seam, for example when knitting a throw. There are many different ways to cast on, but one of the following two methods is suitable for most knitting. If you tend to cast on too tightly, use a slightly thicker needle than for the main fabric.

Making a slip loop (see opposite)

This is always the first casting-on stage, as both cable cast-on and thumb cast-on start with a slip loop.

I Wrap the yarn once around the fingers of your left hand, holding the end with your thumb. Wrap the yarn around your fingers again, making sure you cross the second strand over the first.
2 Insert a knitting needle under the first strand and over the second. Hooking the second strand with the tip of the needle, draw it underneath and up through the loop.
3 With the needle through the loop, pull the short end of yarn to tighten the knot as you slide the loop off your fingers.
4 Continue tightening the knot by pulling the other end of the yarn, closing the knot up close to the needle.

Cable cast-on (see page 20)

This cast-on creates a firm, cord-like edge and is made by knitting a stitch, then transferring it from the right needle to the left.

I Make a slip loop on the left needle, then insert the right needle into the front of it and pass the yarn around the tip of the needle.
2 Draw it through to create a new stitch on the right needle.
3 Now transfer the newly formed stitch to the left needle.
4 Gently pull the yarn to tighten it and then secure the stitch on the needle.
5 Insert the right needle between the two stitches and then pass the yarn around the right needle.
6 Draw the yarn through to create a new stitch and put it on the left needle.

Repeat steps 5 and 6 until the required number of stitches have been cast on.

Thumb cast-on (see page 21)

This cast-on is more elastic so is suitable for ribbed fabrics. Because of its construction it is almost invisible on garter stitch. One needle is used and the stitches are knitted off your thumb.

I Make a slip loop on the needle at a distance 3 times the length of the edge to be cast on from the end. Hold the needle in the right hand along with the yarn attached to the ball.
2 With the other end held under tension in your left hand, make a loop around your thumb and insert the needle under the yarn into the loop.
3 Pass the ball end of the yarn around the needle using your right-hand index finger.
4 Draw a loop through to make a stitch, and then pull the short end of the yarn to close the stitch up to the needle.

Repeat steps 2–4 until the required number of stitches are cast on.

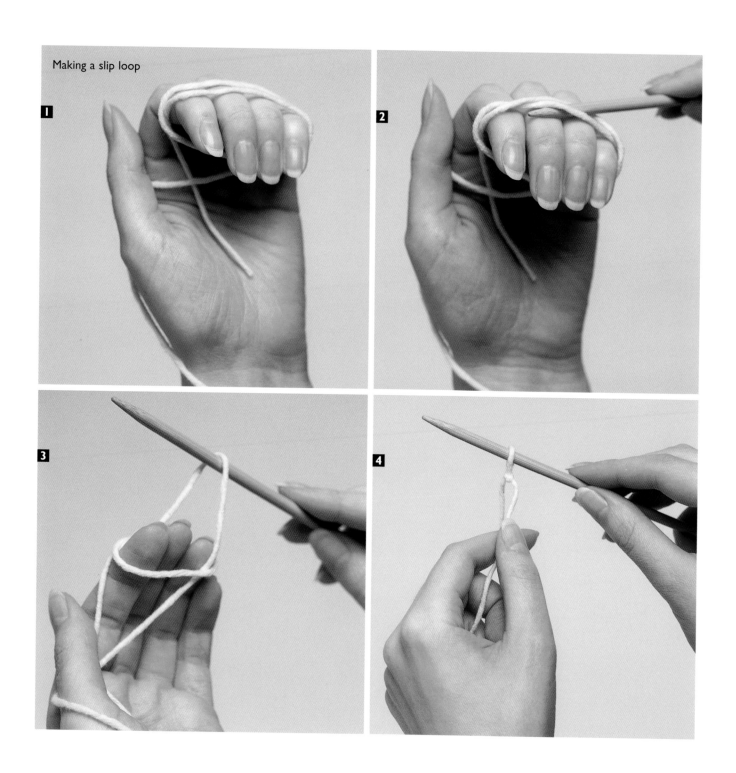

Making a slip loop

1

2

3

4

Cable cast-on

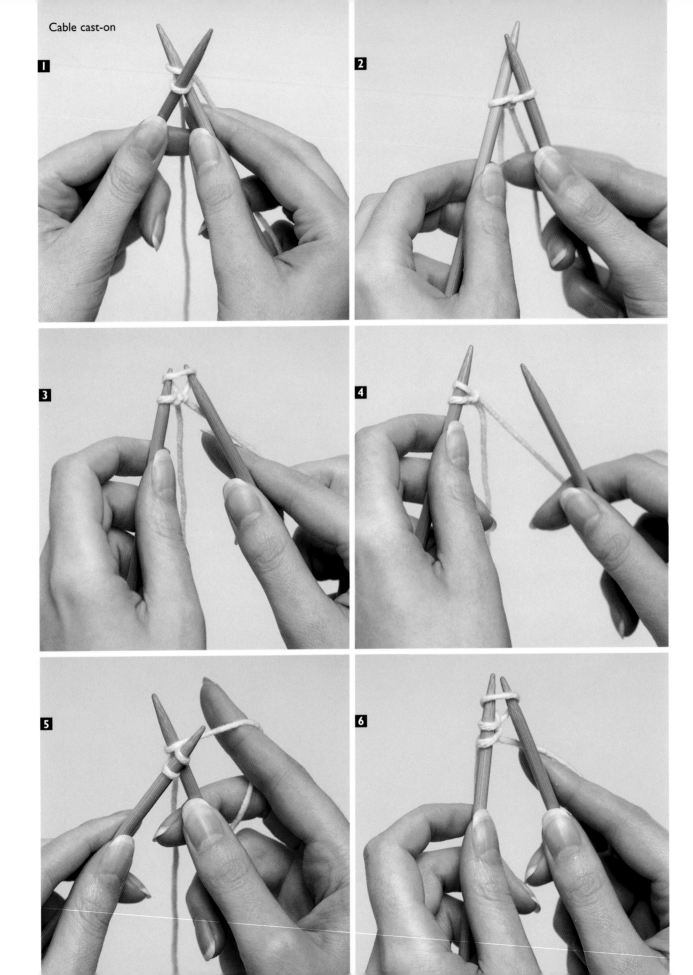

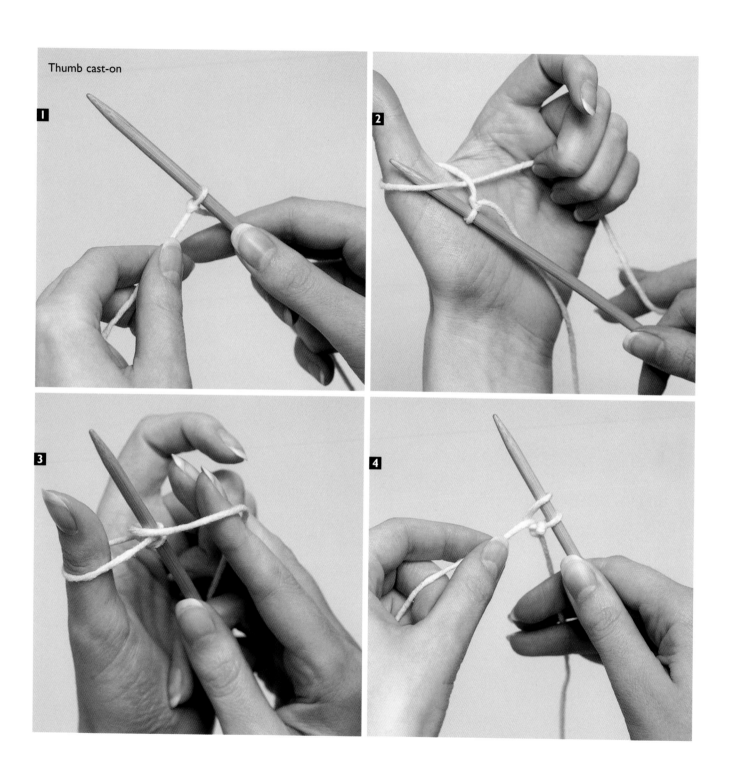

Thumb cast-on

1

2

3

4

Casting off

Casting off secures the stitches when a piece of work is complete, linking them together so that the knitting cannot unravel. Chain cast-off is the most basic method, where each stitch is knitted before being passed through the previous one. Fabrics are usually cast off in stitch (following the sequence of knit and purl stitches of the pattern being knitted), unless a special effect is required. Casting off can be done with a slightly thicker needle to prevent the edge being too tight and pulling the fabric in. Achieving an even tension in order to create a neat row of evenly sized loops along the edge can take some practice.

Chain cast-off

Drawing each stitch through the previous one creates a chain along the top edge of the knitting that is visible on the side from which it is worked.

Casting off in knit

It is usual to cast off knitwise, meaning on a knit row of stocking stitch, unless stated otherwise.

1 Work 2 stitches following the pattern you have been working. Then, using the left needle, lift the first stitch over the second.
2 Let the first stitch fall off the needle leaving a single stitch on the right needle.
3 Work another stitch so that there are 2 stitches on the right needle, then lift the first over the second and off the needle.
4 Repeat step 3 until there is only 1 stitch remaining on the right needle and none on the left. Cut the yarn, pass it through the remaining stitch and pull it tight.

Casting off in purl

Work in the same way as for knit, but the yarn will now be sitting in front of the work rather than behind.

1 Work 2 purl stitches so that they are sitting on the right needle.
2 Lift the first stitch over the second and then off the needle. Continue in the same way as for casting off in knit until there is only 1 stitch remaining on the right needle. Now cut the yarn, pass it through the remaining stitch and pull it tight.

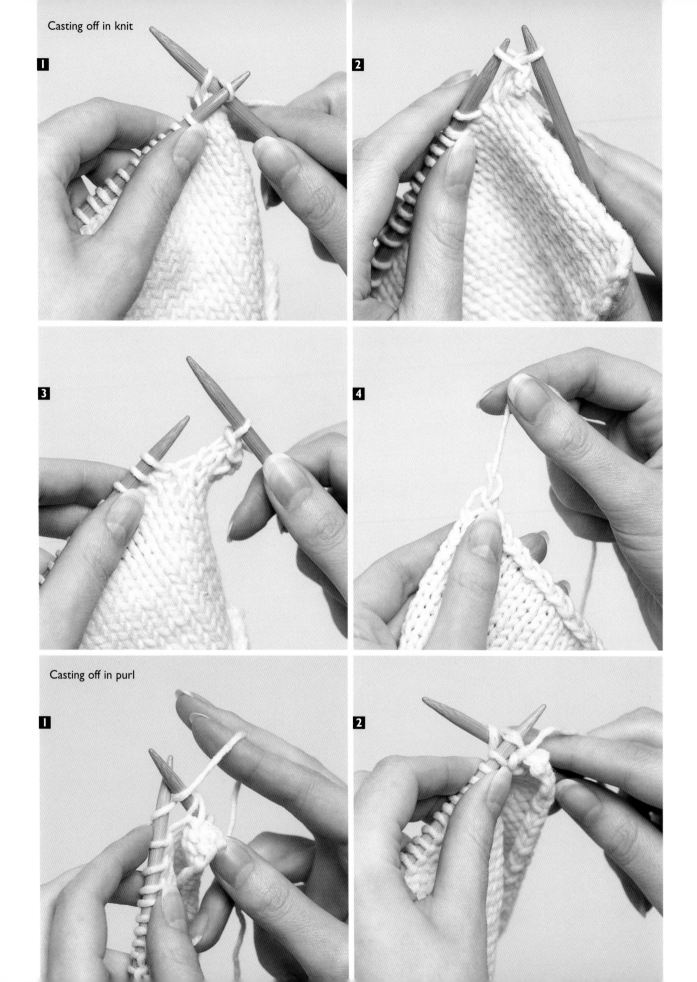

Casting off in knit

1

2

3

4

Casting off in purl

1

2

23

Understanding tension

Tension is a way to describe the size of the stitch within a knitted fabric, expressed as the number of stitches and rows over a given measurement – usually 10cm (4in) square. This depends on the thickness of the yarn, the thickness of the needle, the stitch type and how much yarn the knitter puts into each stitch. If a fabric is too loose, it will be very open, with uneven stitches; if it is too tight, the stitches will be densely packed and the fabric stiff. In general, thicker yarn is best knitted with thicker needles, but the pattern designer will have worked out the optimum tension to make a fabric with a good appearance and suitable handle for the design.

Knitting with a slightly tighter tension than usual will increase the stability of the fabric, which is usually advantageous when knitting soft furnishings. So try to match the tension of your fabric to that stated in the knitting pattern by adjusting the needle up or down a size if required. When the number of stitches and rows stays constant, variation in tension also affects the size of the finished fabric. The pictures opposite show the same yarn knitted on 4½mm (no 7/US 7) and 5½mm (no 5/US 9) needles, the thinnest and thickest needles recommended for this yarn to produce a usable fabric. Both squares have the same number of stitches and rows but the dimensions and appearance of the fabrics are quite different. Knitted on a finer needle the fabric is much firmer and the dimensions are smaller. The good news is that for the soft-furnishing designs in this book, variation in size is not as important as

it is for clothing. If the tension does not differ wildly from that given in the instructions, the fabric will look and feel acceptable. It will not matter if a throw is slightly larger or smaller than expected, while a cushion pad can be selected to fit the size of the cover. The most important thing for a beginner is to try to keep the tension in the knitting consistent so that the fabric is even.

Some yarns are best knitted loosely (fluffy, loopy and chenille yarns, for example), while yarns with a high amount of twist benefit from being tightly knitted. Until you are a fairly confident knitter, it is wisest to use the same yarn as stated in the pattern. To check that your knitting will have the correct tension, knit a piece of fabric at least 12cm (4¾in) square in just the same stitch as the pattern. In fact, the larger the swatch, the more accurate the measurement will be.

After blocking the swatch as you would the finished article, mark an area exactly 10cm (4in) square in the centre. The cast-on and cast-off edges should be disregarded because they are often distorted and would affect the accuracy of your calculation. Count the number of stitches and rows within the marked area. If you have more stitches than in your pattern, try using a thicker needle; if you have fewer, try using a finer needle. The number of stitches and rows per cm (or inch) given on a yarn band has been taken from stocking-stitch fabric (alternate rows of knit and purl) and it is usual for there to be more rows than stitches. This is because all stitches, other than those that have been double-wrapped or held, are wider than they are tall. This is exaggerated in garter-stitch fabrics where, because the stitches lie at an angle within the fabric structure, there tends to be about twice the number of rows as stitches.

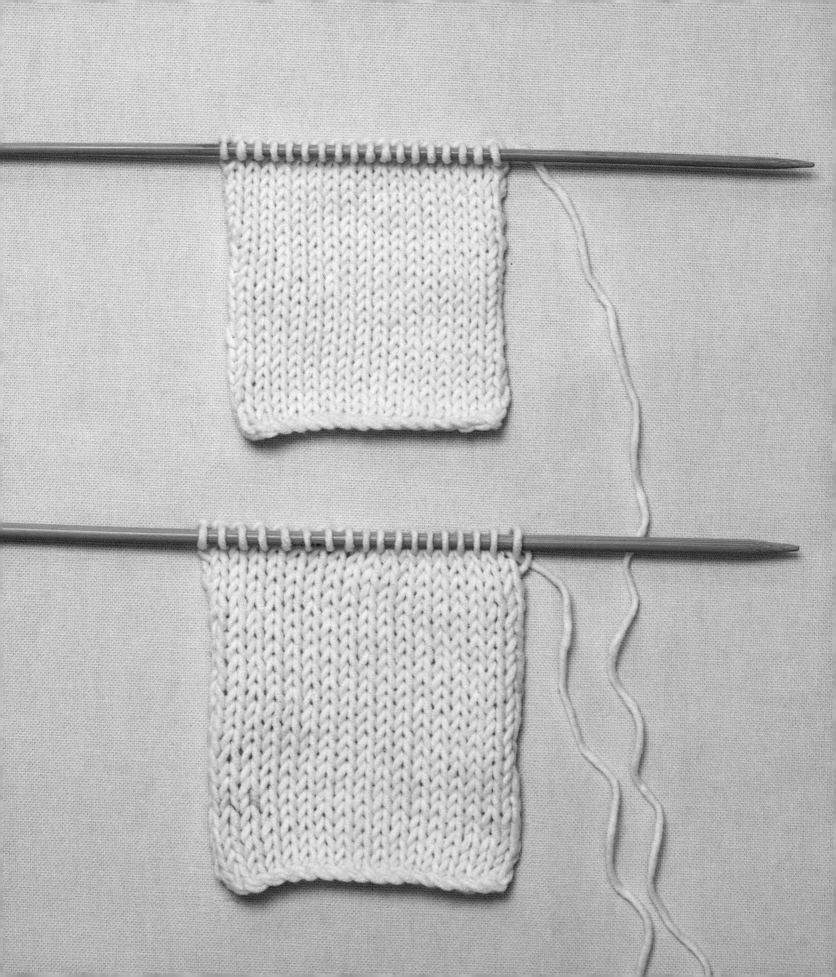

Holding the needles and yarn

Find a way of holding the yarn and needles that is comfortable – this will make knitting more enjoyable and the fabrics that you produce more even. There are many ways of holding the needles and yarn, with methods often associated with particular countries and geographical regions. The right needle can be held over the top or from underneath, resting in the crook of the thumb and index finger. The yarn can also be held in either the left or right hand, with each requiring a slightly different knitting action. Here, the yarn is always shown held in the right hand. Either technique can be used as long as the path of the yarn around the needles remains the same.

Holding the right needle as a pen
The left needle is held over the top and controlled with the thumb and index finger. The right needle is held as a pen. This is supposed to be the more elegant way to hold the needles, but fabric tends to gather in the crook of the thumb.

Holding the needle with the hand on top
The left needle is held over the top and controlled with the thumb and index finger. The right needle is held with the hand on top. This is a good method to use when knitting larger pieces of work.

Holding the yarn
The yarn can be held in a number of different ways, to tension it during knitting. Try this method to begin with.

Hold the yarn in the right hand, take it over the index finger, weave it under and over the other fingers and finish under the little finger. The yarn is then passed around the needle with the index finger, and the little finger grips the yarn to keep its tension. The yarn can also circle the little finger to keep it under tension.

The face or right side of the fabric is the side that is intended to be mainly on view; this can be more obvious with some fabrics than with others. A Fair Isle definitely has a right side on which the pattern is clearly seen, with the floats appearing on the wrong side. Knit-and-purl textured patterns can be completely reversible (good for throws and blankets, as both sides will be seen). Where the two sides are different, either could be used as the right side – sometimes it is only a matter of preference.

As knitting progresses, the stitches pass from needle to needle, and at the end of each row the work is turned so that either the right side or the wrong side of the fabric will be facing you. A row where the right side of the fabric is facing you as you knit is referred to as a right-side row, whereas a row where the wrong side is facing you is a wrong-side row.

Reading patterns
Read the pattern through before starting, in order to get a general understanding of it. Abbreviations are used for many words that appear repeatedly. Not all patterns use the same abbreviations but the ones most often used for each different type of stitch are given in the appropriate sections of this book. There are also some general abbreviations that it will help to know:

alt – alternate(ly)   beg – begin(ning)
cont – continue   foll – follow
patt – pattern   rep – repeat

Most knitted designs involve considerable repetition, both horizontally across the stitches in a row and vertically from row to row. To make the instructions as concise as possible, brackets and asterisks are used.

(_ _ _) – repeat the instructions inside the brackets as many times as indicated after the brackets.
_ – repeat the instructions between the asterisks as many more times as indicated. To make balanced, symmetrical designs, rows must begin and end in the same way, hence the instructions will often have a number of extra stitches outside the brackets or asterisks.

Holding the right needle as a pen

Holding the needle with the hand on top

Holding the yarn

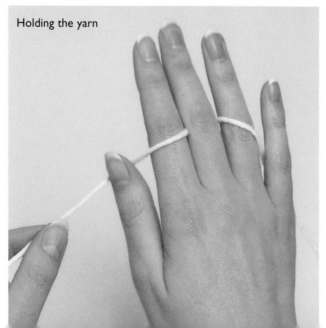

Basic Stitches

Knitting is a succession of interlocking waves

of yarn, formed by looping the yarn over a needle. The loop is drawn through the previous stitch, which is then slipped off the needle, forming a new stitch above. The bottom of each new wave interlocks with the top of the wave below. Needles are used to keep the loops in place and to make them a constant size. If you unravel a piece of fabric that has been knitted for some time, you will see that the yarn is no longer straight, but crinkled, having been set in its wavy path.

Knit and purl are basically the two sides of a stitch. When the needle is inserted from the front to the back of a loop and the yarn passed around the back, a knit stitch is formed. This shows the knit side of the stitch on the side of the fabric that is facing you. If the needle is inserted from the back to the front of a loop and the yarn passed around the front, a purl stitch will be formed. This shows the purl side of the stitch on the side of the fabric facing you. The work normally progresses from the right to the left. The yarn hangs from the needle in the right hand while the needle in the left hand holds the stitches worked in the previous row. All knitting patterns, from plain stocking stitch to cables or the most complicated multicoloured patterns, are based on these two basic stitches.

Knit stitch

A knit stitch is a stitch formed with the interlocking side facing away from you as you knit. When every stitch of every row is a knit stitch, garter-stitch fabric is produced. Both sides of this fabric are the same, with strong horizontal ridges, each ridge being made by two rows of stitches. One row forms a smooth line on the side facing you and a raised bar on the other side. Then, because the piece is turned at the end of the row, the raised bar shows on the face of the next row and the smooth line on the other side. The stitches lie at an angle within the fabric, so the width of one stitch is usually roughly equal in size to two rows and it takes a lot of rows to knit a given length. This also makes it a bulky fabric that is very stretchy lengthways unless it is worked firmly with needles one or two sizes smaller than usual. Although this is the most basic knitted fabric, its very individual characteristics make it extremely useful. Because alternate rows pull in opposite directions, it does not curl, making it a suitable stitch for borders.

1 Taking the needle with the stitches in the left hand and with the yarn to the back, insert the right needle through the front of the stitch, from left to right.
2 Pass the yarn from left to right, under and up the front of the point of the right needle.
3 Draw the yarn through the stitch to make a loop on the right needle.
4 Drop the original stitch from the left needle at the same time, creating a new stitch on the right needle.

To knit a whole row, repeat steps 1–4 until all the stitches are on the right needle. Turn the piece, transferring the needle with the stitches to your left hand so that the side that was the back of the piece is now facing you. You are ready to start knitting the next row.

The traditional way to remember the four basic steps that create a knitted stitch are: 'in', 'round', 'through' and 'off'.

Pattern instructions

A knit stitch would be written in a pattern as 'K', followed by the number of stitches to be knitted, e.g 'K1', 'K14' or 'K to end' for a whole row of knit stitches. The following two projects have been written out in full to help you while you master the basics.

The steps should soon start to flow into each other as you increase in confidence and speed. When you become more experienced, keep the stitches being worked nearer the tip of the needle. Keep the yarn between the piece and your finger quite short and try to flick the yarn around the needle without moving your finger too far. This will speed up your knitting while keeping the stitches even.

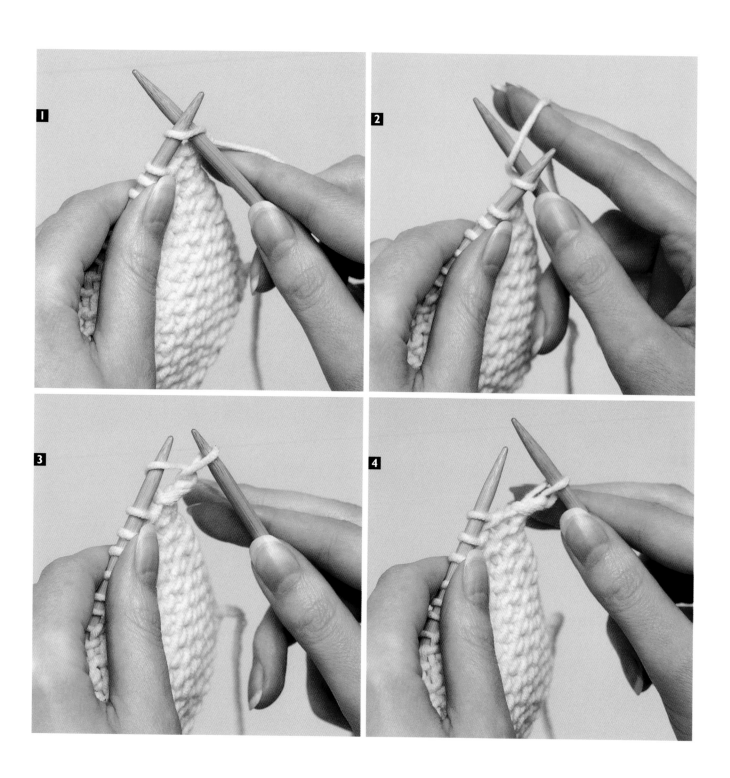

Woven-strip cushion The pronounced horizontal ridges of garter stitch emphasize the woven construction of this cushion cover. Strips are interlaced at right angles to create a highly textured, chequered effect. Worked in charcoal and flannel grey, the look is sophisticated and monochrome, but you could also try using a number of different bright or pastel colours for more of a 'patchwork' effect.

You will need

Pair of 4mm (no 8/US 6) knitting needles

5 x 50g (1¾oz) balls of dk [short for double knitting] merino wool yarn in charcoal (A)

3 x 50g (1¾oz) balls of dk merino wool yarn in flannel grey (B)

Sewing needle and pins

3 buttons

45cm (18in) square cushion pad

Tension

22 stitches and 40 rows over 10cm (4in) square of garter stitch

Finished size

45cm (18in) square

Working the cushion cover front

With 4mm (no 8/US 6) needles and Yarn A, cast on 11 stitches.
1st row: Knit to end.
Repeating this row makes garter stitch.
Knit 180 rows of garter stitch.
Cast off.
Work 8 more strips as above in Yarn A, and 9 strips in Yarn B.

Working the cushion cover back

The cover back is worked in 2 pieces.
First piece With 4mm (no 8/US 6) needles and Yarn A, cast on 99 stitches.
Knit 90 rows of garter stitch.
Cast off.
Second piece With 4mm (no 8/US 6) needles and Yarn A, cast on 99 stitches.
Knit 114 rows of garter stitch.
Cast off.

To improve the appearance of the edges of your piece, slip the first stitch of every row. This means simply passing the stitch from the left to the right needle without knitting it, then knit the rest of the stitches as usual (see pages 90–1 for instructions on slip stitch). Remember that when counting the number of rows knitted, each ridge is 2 rows.

Making up the cushion cover

1 Press and block all the pieces to size. Each strip should measure 5 x 45cm (2 x 18in). Lay the 2 back pieces right side up, with the smaller piece uppermost, overlapping them in the middle by 6cm (2½in). Pin the 2 pieces together at the overlap so that the resulting piece measures 45cm (18in) square.
2 Lay the charcoal strips vertically, edge to edge on top, right sides down. Line up the top ends of the strips with the top edge of the back and pin in place along the top edge.
3 Do the same with the flannel-grey strips, lining up their ends with the left side of the back piece, and pin along that edge only.
4 Weave the first flannel-grey strip alternately under then over the charcoal strips and pin the strip to the back piece at the opposite side. Weave the next strip alternately over then under and pin at the other side.
5 When all the strips are woven together, pin the charcoal strips edge to edge along the bottom of the back piece.
6 Backstitch the ends of the strips to the back piece, around all 4 edges. Turn right sides out.
7 Work 3 loops across the edge of the uppermost back piece, and sew buttons underneath to match them. Insert the cushion pad and button the cover closed.

Superchunky knit throw This generous throw, knitted in simple garter stitch, creates a full, spongy fabric that would be wondrously cosy on a chilly day. Big, thick needles and superchunky yarn make it very quick to knit, while the irregularity of the yarn means there are no worries about the size and evenness of the stitches. A ribbon edging holds the throw in shape and gives it a traditional blanket feel.

You will need

Pair of 15mm (US 19)
knitting needles

10 x 100g (3½oz) hanks
of superchunky slub yarn
in damson

4.5m (15ft) of 39mm (1½in)
wide navy taffeta ribbon

Sewing needle and pins

Tension

6.5 stitches and 12 rows
over 10cm (4in) square
of garter stitch

Finished size

100 x 120cm (39½ x 47¼in)

Working the throw

With 15mm (US 19) needles, cast on a total
of 66 stitches.
1st row: Knit to end.
Repeating this row makes garter stitch.
Knit 144 rows or until work measures 120cm
(47¼in) from the cast-on edge.
Cast off.

Where each new ball of yarn has been
joined in, loosely knot the ends together, then
sew them in when your knitting is complete.
As the edges are to be covered with ribbon,
an edge is the best place at which to join in
a new ball, but because the row is quite long
and the yarn superchunky, you may want to
do this part of the way along a row to avoid
wasting too much yarn. Try to finish and start
where the yarn is at its finest to make the
ends easier to sew into the fabric afterwards.

Making up the throw

1 Press and block the piece to size, then finish
the edges with ribbon.
2 Cut the ribbon to a length of 4m 43cm
(14½ft), iron it in half lengthways and
backstitch the 2 ends together 1.5cm (⅝in)
from the end to form a continuous loop.
3 Starting with the join as the first corner,
mark the other 3 corner points 100cm
(39½in), 120cm (47¼in) and 100cm (39½in)
apart. Backstitch a mitre at each of these
points (see page 143).
4 Matching the mitred corners to the
appropriate corners of the throw, pin, tack
and stitch the ribbon in place using running
stitch, so that the throw is sandwiched
between the 2 layers of folded ribbon.
Your throw is now complete.

Purl stitch

Purl is a knit stitch formed back to front so that the interlocking side of the stitch faces you as you knit. If every row were purled, the resulting fabric would be garter stitch just as with knit stitch, but when alternate rows of knit and purl are worked, stocking-stitch fabric is produced. It is smooth on one side, showing the v-shaped bases of the stitches, and bumpy on the other, showing the horizontal bars at the top of the stitches. The bumpy side looks similar to garter stitch but flatter, and when used as the right side of the fabric it is referred to as reverse stocking stitch. It is more usual, however, to use the smoother side as the right side.

Stocking stitch is the most widely knitted fabric because it is finer and more stable than garter stitch. This is the fabric referred to on yarn labels when giving a recommended tension, against which other fabrics are compared. It forms the basis of most colourwork such as Fair Isle and intarsia because the cleanly outlined stitches on the right side of the fabric and the flat, regular surface make well-defined patterns. Stocking-stitch fabric does not naturally lie flat: it curls out at the top and bottom but in at the sides, so fabrics need to be well pressed. Free edges will usually be finished with a different stitch or sometimes left to curl intentionally.

1 Taking the needle with the stitches in the left hand and keeping the yarn to the front, insert the right needle through the front of the first stitch, from right to left.
2 Pass the yarn from right to left, over and down behind the point of the right needle.
3 Draw the yarn through the stitch to make a loop on the right needle.
4 Drop the original stitch from the left needle at the same time, creating a new stitch on the right needle.

To purl a whole row, repeat steps 1–4 until all the stitches are on the right needle. Turn the piece, transferring the needle with the stitches to your left hand. The side that was the back of the piece will now be facing you. You are ready to start the next row, which if you were knitting stocking stitch would be a row of knit stitches.

The selvedges are the outer stitches of each row that form the vertical sides of the knitting. To keep them neat and minimize bagginess, knit the first few stitches of each row tightly, particularly the purl stitches. Alternatively, slip the first stitch of each row to put less yarn into these areas.

Pattern instructions
A purl stitch would be written on a pattern as 'P', followed by the number of stitches to be purled, e.g. 'P1' or 'P14'. When a pattern includes a number of alternating knit and purl rows, called stocking stitch, this can be written as 'st st' then followed by the number of rows and the type of row with which to start knitting, e.g. '4 rows st st starting with a K row' means knit 1 row, purl 1 row, knit 1 row, purl 1 row. The following two projects have been written out in full to help you while you master the basics.

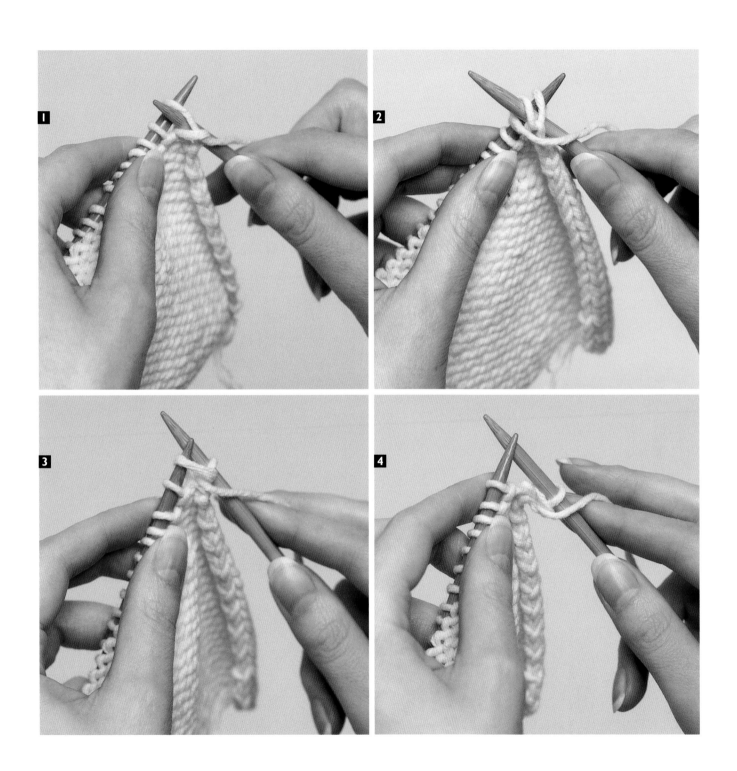

Corner-folded cushion Wrap your cushion in a square of soft merino wool and fasten the four corners together at the front with a button to make a simple, contemporary cover. The open edges allow a glimpse of the cushion beneath, which can be covered in fabric of a toning or contrasting colour. Choose a large button to make an arresting centrepiece to the flower shape formed by the opening.

You will need

Pair of 15mm (US 19) knitting needles

320g (11oz) hank of merino roving in raspberry ripple

Sewing needle and pins

1 large button

50cm (20in) square cushion pad with pink fabric cover

Tension

8 stitches and 9 rows over 10cm (4in) square of stocking stitch

Finished size

71cm (28in) square folded to 50cm (20in) square

Working the cushion cover

The cushion cover is knitted in a single piece, 71cm (28in) square.
With 15mm (US 19) needles, cast on a total of 56 stitches.
1st row: Knit to end.
2nd row: Purl to end.
The formation of these 2 rows make stocking stitch.
Work a total of 64 rows of stocking stitch or until the piece measures 71cm (28in) from the cast-on edge.
Cast off.

Making up the cushion cover

1 Press and block the piece to size. Laying the square right side down, fold all four corners to the centre, then pin and oversew 4 seams, catching only half of a stitch along each side, halfway to the centre.

2 Oversew 3 of the corners together at the centre and then work a loop fastening (see pages 143–5 for instructions) catching all 3 layers. Sew the button at the fourth corner. To complete the cushion, insert the cushion pad and button the cover closed.

Chequered cube A patchwork of natural-coloured wools makes a contemporary yet hardwearing cover for a seating cube. Extra texture is created by alternating between the smoother knit and the rougher purl sides of the stocking-stitch fabric, while raised, oversewn seams give added definition. To adapt the look use strongly contrasting colours or knit all the squares in the same colour to emphasize the different textures.

You will need

Pair of 5mm (no 6/US 8) knitting needles

150g (5oz) cone of Aran yarn in dark beige (A)

150g (5oz) cone of Aran yarn in light beige (B)

150g (5oz) cone of Aran yarn in ecru (C)

170g (6oz) cone of Aran yarn in beige marl (D)

Sewing needle and pins

45 x 45 x 45cm (18 x 18 x 18in) block of 33/190 grade foam

Tension

16 stitches and 20½ rows over 10cm (4in) square of stocking stitch

Finished size

45 x 45 x 45cm (18 x 18 x 18in)

Working the squares

With 5mm (no 6/US 8) needles and Yarn A, cast on 38 stitches.
1st row: Knit to end.
2nd row: Purl to end.
These 2 rows make stocking stitch. Work a total of 46 rows of stocking stitch.
Cast off.
Work 5 more squares as above in Yarn A to make a total of 6 squares.
Work 6 squares as above in Yarns B, C and D.

Making up the cube cover

1 Press and block all of the 24 squares to size. Each finished pieces should measure 24cm (9½in) square.
2 Arrange the squares in the order shown in the diagram. Colours B and D have the stocking-stitch side of the fabric showing, while colours A and C have the reverse stocking-stitch side showing. The direction of the rows is indicated by the horizontal and vertical arrows.
3 Using Yarn D, oversew the seams with wrong sides together so that the edges are visible on the right side (see page 142 for instructions). Begin by oversewing the squares together in twos, then oversew these together into groups of 4.

4 Oversew 5 of these large composite squares together to form an open-ended cube. Slip the cover over the foam inner and oversew the final side in place.

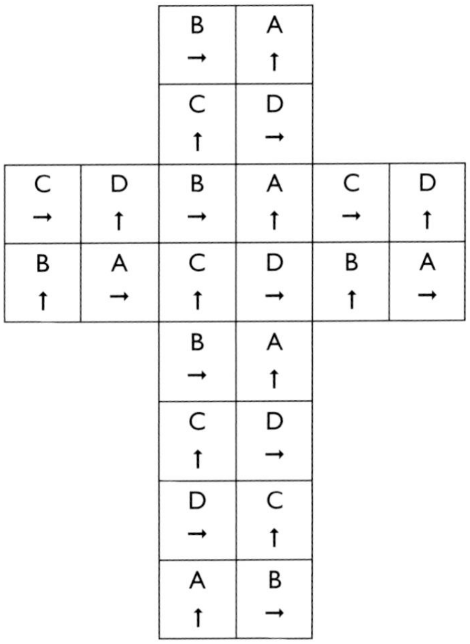

Knit-and-purl patterns

Textured patterns can be knitted by forming stitches with sometimes the knit side and sometimes the purl side visible on the right side of the fabric. The surfaces of the two are very different in nature, the knit stitch being smooth and tending to reflect light, the raised bar of the purl stitch being bumpy and broken and tending to absorb light. Vertical rows of knit and purl stitches, called ribs, are one of the simplest ways to create a textured fabric by combining the two. By varying the number of stitches before taking the yarn back to knit or bringing it forward to purl, a whole variety of different ribs can be formed.

Ribbed fabric is more springy and elastic across its width than stocking stitch, and the narrower the rib, the more tightly the fabric will pull in. This elasticity helps the fabric to keep its shape, making it a good choice for borders. When the yarn is moved from the front to the back, the fabric is loosened, which can create a flared effect. Consequently the rib is often worked on a smaller size of needle to make it firmer, particularly if the main work is in a firm stitch. To cast off in rib, knit each stitch as you would a normal row, before lifting the first stitch over the second and off the needle. Take the yarn back or bring it forward to change between a knit and purl in the usual way.

Single rib has unbroken vertical lines of alternating knit and purl stitches with the same appearance on both sides of the piece. Stitches that have been knitted on the first row are purled on the next, and those that are purled on the first row are knitted on the next. Because the fabric is turned around between rows, the stitches above each other all face in the same direction, therefore forming vertical lines.

Double rib is another commonly used rib, formed when 2 stitches are knitted and then 2 are purled. This type of rib will draw in less than a single rib.

1 Knit the first stitch with the yarn at the back of the work to form a normal knit stitch.
2 Bring the yarn between the needles to the front of the work.
3 Purl the next stitch.
4 Take the yarn between the needles to the back of the work and knit a knit stitch.

Repeat steps 2 and 3 until all the stitches have been worked and are on the right-hand needle. Your first row of rib is now complete. On the subsequent rows all the stitches that were knitted on the previous row should be purled and all those that were purled should be knitted.

Pattern instructions
Over an even number of stitches this would be written on a pattern as:
1st row: (K1, P1) to end.
or sometimes
1st row: *K1, P1, rep from * to end.
Over an odd number of stitches the rows begin alternately with a knit and a purl stitch so that they line up correctly; this would be written on a pattern as:
1st row: K1, (P1, K1) to end.
2nd row: P1, (K1, P1) to end, or
1st row: (K1, P1) to last stitch, K1.
2nd row: (P1, K1) to last stitch, P1, or
1st row: K1, *P1, K1, rep from * to end.
2nd row: P1, *K1, P1, rep from * to end.

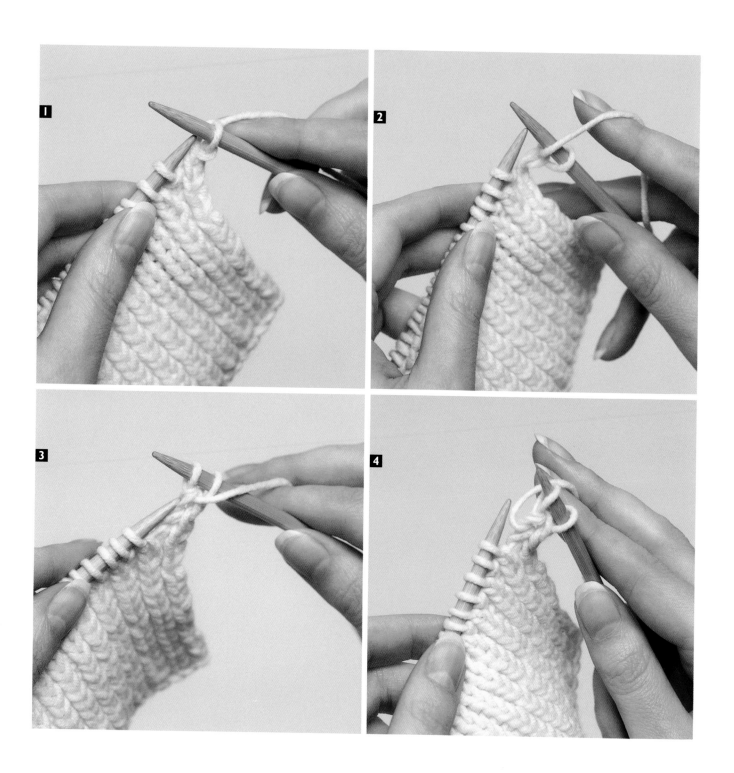

Button-edged rib cushion Ribs in varying widths make an elegantly textured surface of vertical lines through the interchange of the raised, smooth knit and recessed, lumpy purl stitches on one side. Changing the width of the ribs produces an interesting graded effect. The pronounced lines created where the knit stitches stand proud from the purl stitches can be softened by using lustrous, hairy mohair yarn or emphasized by using a smooth, crisp cotton yarn. The buttons are an important element so choose them in an interesting material, colour and shape that complements the yarn. These pewter-finish buttons are sixteenth-century reproductions.

You will need
Pair of 5mm (no 6/US 8) knitting needles

Pair of 4.5mm (no 7/US 7) knitting needles

4 x 50g (1¾oz) balls of lambswool/mohair/nylon blend yarn in pale grey

Sewing needle and pins

4 buttons

45cm (18in) square cushion pad

Tension
18 stitches and 25 rows over 10cm (4in) square of stocking stitch

Finished size
45 x 48cm (18 x 19in)

Working the cushion cover back
With 5mm (no 6/US 8) needles, cast on a total of 86 stitches.
1st row: P2, K8, P2, K6, P2, (K4, P2) twice, (K2, P2) 6 times, (K4, P2) twice, K6, P2, K8 P2.
2nd row: K2, P8, K2, P6, K2, (P4, K2) twice, (P2, K2) 6 times, (P4, K2) twice, P6, K2, P8 K2.
Rep 1st and 2nd rows until the piece measures 45cm (18in), finishing on a right-side row (approximately 111 rows).
Button band 1st row: K to end.
Change to 4.5mm (no 7/US 7) needles.
2nd row: K2, (P2, K2) to end.
3rd row: P2, (K2, P2) to end.
Rep 2nd and 3rd rows 4 more times.
Cast off in rib.

Working the cushion cover front
Work a second piece the same as the back, up to the button band.
Button band 1st row: K to end.
Change to 4.5mm (no 7/US 7) needles.
2nd row: K2, (P2, K2) to end.
3rd row: P2, (K2, P2) to end.
Rep 2nd and 3rd rows once more.
1st buttonhole row: (K2, P2) 3 times, *cast off 2 sts, P2, (K2, P2) 4 times *, rep from * to * twice more, cast off 2 sts, (P2, K2) 3 times.
2nd buttonhole row: (P2, K2) 3 times, *cast on 2 sts, K2, (P2, K2) 4 times *, rep from * to * twice more, cast on 2 sts, (K2, P2) 3 times.
Rep 2nd and 3rd button-band rows (with no buttonholes) twice more.
Cast off in rib.

Making up the cushion cover
1 Press and block the front and back pieces to size. With right sides together, pin then backstitch the pieces together around 3 edges, leaving the button-band edge open.
2 Turn the cover right sides out and sew buttons on the inside of the back-button band to correspond with the buttonholes on the front. Insert the cushion pad and button the cover closed.

Alternative knit-and-purl patterns

Varying the individual configurations of knit and purl stitches from row to row can create a wide range of textures and is the basis of many knitting patterns. Knit areas will stand up from purl in a vertical design, as can be seen on ribbed fabrics, but they will recede where a design has horizontal elements. This can be clearly seen when rows of stocking stitch are followed by rows of reverse stocking stitch to produce raised ridges called welts on the final piece. This also applies to figurative designs where there are elements of both, sometimes with quite pronounced results.

Knit and purl stitches can be arranged to form repeating designs such as moss stitch (seed stitch), blocks, diamonds, basket weaves and chevrons. They can also form individual motifs set against a background, which is usually worked in stocking stitch to emphasize the different textures. The differences in the knit and purl sides of the stitch are accentuated by using a plain yarn with a smooth, regular quality in a light colour. Knitting with a reasonably tight tension will also make the detail in the designs much clearer. When you are reading a chart, think of the empty squares as the smooth surface of knit stitches and the dots as the bumpy bar-like appearance of the purl stitches on the right side of the fabric.

Working moss stitch

Moss stitch is a commonly used knit-and-purl textured pattern. It consists of alternating knit and purl stitches in a chequered arrangement, achieved by knit stitches being knitted and purl stitches being purled on every row. The resultant fabric has a dotty, broken appearance on both the right side and wrong side and does not stretch or curl, making moss stitch an excellent choice for edgings.

Knit a row of K1, P1, repeating to the end of the row. Do the same in the next row, but instead of forming a purl above a knit and a knit above a purl as you would do to achieve a single rib, form a knit above a knit stitch and a purl above a purl. Because the fabric has been turned between rows, the characteristic chequered texture is created.

Pattern instructions

Moss stitch would usually be worked over an odd number of stitches and could be written on a pattern as:

1st row: K1, (P1, K1) to end.

Over an even number of stitches it could be written as:

1st row: (K1, P1) to end.

2nd row: (P1, K1) to end.

More complicated knit-and-purl designs are given in chart form, with a square representing a stitch. This gives a better overview of the design than written instructions would, as it can then be seen at a glance how one row relates to the next. Symbols are used to represent knit and purl stitches – usually an empty square represents a knit stitch on right-side rows and a purl on wrong-side rows, while a square with a dot represents a purl stitch on right-side rows and a knit stitch on wrong-side rows. There are also different symbols to represent cables, slip stitches, increases and decreases. In fact, any stitch type can be represented in chart form and can be combined with knit and purl stitches. Not all charts use the same symbols, so there will always be a key provided.

The rows in the chart are numbered from the bottom to the top. Right-side rows are read from right to left and wrong-side rows from left to right. Pattern repeats will be marked, and extra stitches, usually at the edges, are sometimes shaded. The number of times that the rows are repeated could be marked on the chart, or instructions could be given in the text. On the chart, designs always appear taller in proportion to their width than they do in fabric form. This is because knitted stitches are wider than they are tall. To achieve a shape of the correct proportions when knitting is finished, the designer will have added extra rows, for example a square may be 4 stitches wide but 6 rows deep.

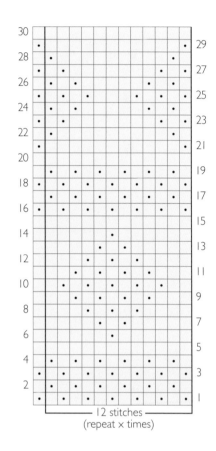

— 12 stitches —
(repeat x times)

☐ K on RS, P on WS rows

⊡ P on RS, K on WS rows

Knit-and-purl baby blanket This blanket, worked in the very softest of snowdrop-white merino wools, has a timeless appeal. The design incorporates moss stitch, with its typical chequered arrangement of knit and purl stitches creating a flat, firm border around the edge of an inviting galaxy of pretty, textured stars. A crisper, summery version of the blanket could be created by using a cotton or cotton-blend yarn.

You will need
Pair of 4mm (no 8/US 6)
knitting needles

7 x 50g (1¾oz) balls of dk
baby merino wool yarn in
snowdrop white

Sewing needle

Tension
22 stitches and 30 rows
over 10cm (4in) square
of stitch pattern

Finished size
87 x 73cm (34¼ x 28½in)

Working the baby blanket
With 4mm (no 8/US 6) needles, cast on a
total of 161 stitches.
Bottom border 1st row: K1 (P1, K1) to end.
Repeat 1st row 7 more times.
Pattern repeat Work 1st to 28th rows of the
pattern-repeat chart (on page 154) 8 times.
Work 1st to 21st rows of pattern-repeat
chart once.

Top border 1st row (wrong-side row):
K1 (P1, K1) to end.
Repeat 1st row 7 more times.
Cast off in moss stitch.
Join in new balls of yarn away from the edges
when they will be visible on the finished
piece, as it is easier to avoid enlarged stitches.

Making up the baby blanket
1 To complete the baby blanket, press and
block the piece to size.

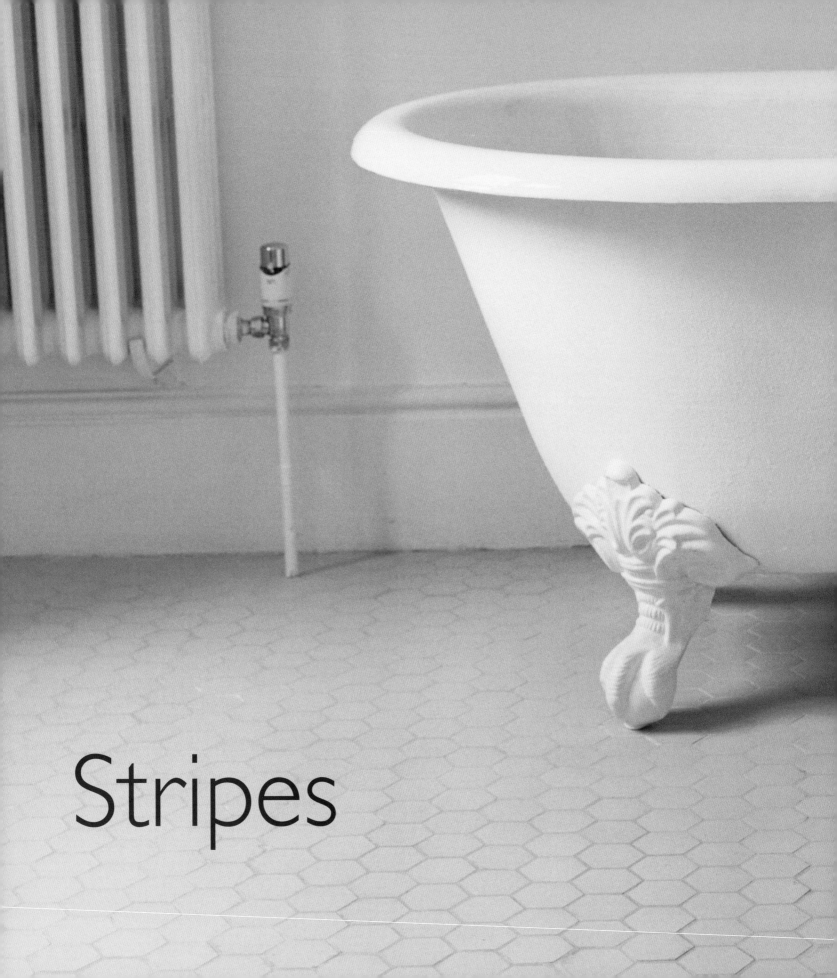

Stripes

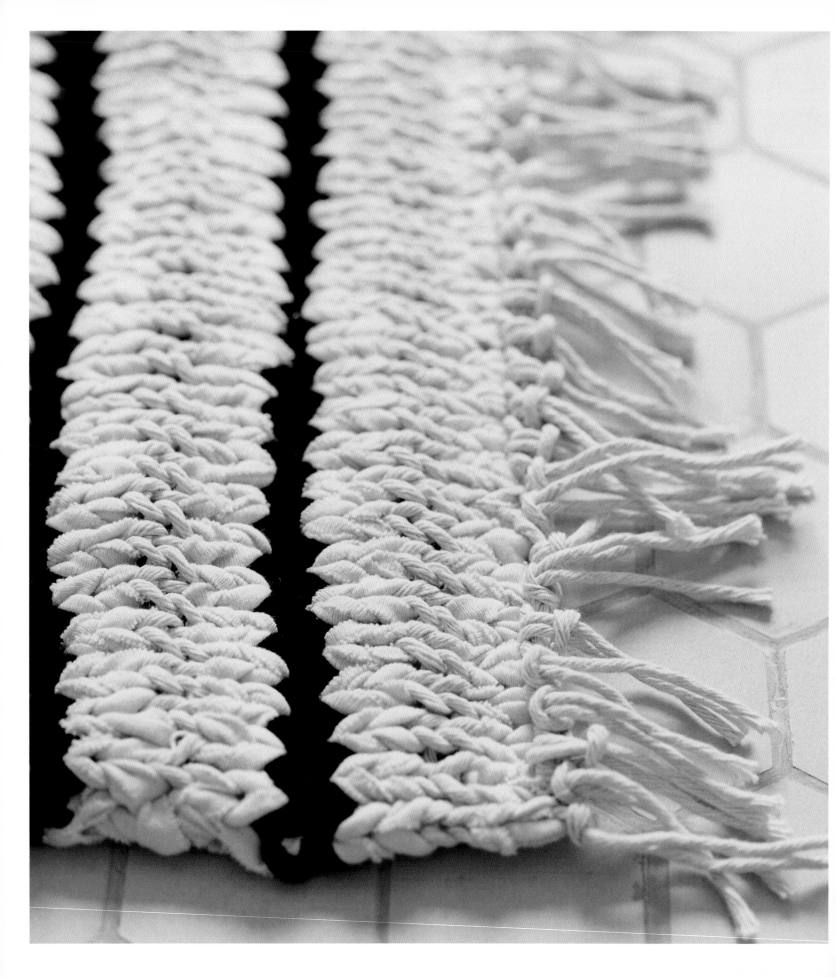

Because knitting is formed in horizontal rows,

it is ideal for striped patterns. Stripes are produced, quite simply, by changing the yarn colour at the start of a new row. Just pick up the new yarn and leave the old yarn hanging. The ends can be loosely tied together and you can tidy them up later. This is the easiest way to knit a multicoloured fabric, because only one yarn is used at a time. There are a limitless number of variations in the size, spacing and proportion of stripes and any stripe sequence can be dramatically transformed by the nature of the colour scheme.

Wide stripes create a colour-blocked effect. A short series of stripes can be repeated over and over or the bands of colour can be totally irregular. With narrow stripes, colours can be carried up the edge of the piece, but take care to wrap the working yarn around those being carried, at intervals of at least 2.5cm (1in), to avoid creating long strands of loose yarn. When knitting wide stripes, knot the new yarn loosely with the old at the end of the row; this will anchor both yarns and avoid enlarged stitches at the edge of the piece. The knot can be untied later and the two ends run through a few stitches on the wrong side of the piece using a wool needle. It is easier to work stripes with an even number of rows so that yarns can be held and colours changed on one edge of the piece.

Striped garter stitch

Apart from varying the depth of the stripe, it is also possible to produce two markedly different-looking stripes depending on the construction of a garter-stitch fabric. If the yarn colour is changed on a wrong-side row, the purl side of the stitch shows on the right side of the fabric and the interlocking bars create a mix of the two colours at the join. As it is usual for the first row to be a right-side row, this happens on even rows. To make a clean stripe, change to a new colour on a right-side row where the knit side of the stitch shows on the right side of the fabric. This will generally happen on odd rows. It is also interesting to note that stripes that are clean on the right side will always be broken on the wrong side of the fabric, and vice versa. However, there is also a technique that alternates between stripes with an odd and even number of rows, and this ensures that both types of stripe can be made to show on the right side of the fabric. Stripes provide an easy way to introduce additional colour to a plain design, as tension is unaffected if the yarn type is the same and the pattern can be followed in the usual way.

1 Changing colour on a right-side (or odd) row, makes a clean-edged colour change on the side facing you.
2 On the wrong side of the fabric, the colour change will have a broken appearance where the intersecting side of the stitches can be seen.
3 Knitting a stripe with an odd number of rows in blue will bring the broken edge colour change to cream to the front of the fabric as the colour change will then take place on a wrong-side (or even) row.

Pattern instructions
Yarns of different types or different colours are assigned a letter (Yarn A, Yarn B, etc.) or sometimes a number (Colour 1, Colour 2, etc.). The colour change for the stripe shown opposite in 1 and 2 would be written on a pattern as:
Yarn A: cream.
Yarn B: blue.
1st to 4th rows: Using Yarn A, K to end.
5th and 6th rows: Using Yarn B, K to end.

If there are a number of different colours in a pattern, make a visual reminder of which yarn is Yarn A, Yarn B, Yarn C, etc. for yourself by sticking a strand of each to the pattern.

Looking at striped fabrics can help in understanding fabric structure in general because it is much easier to see the path of the yarn when it uses a contrasting colour to the previous row.

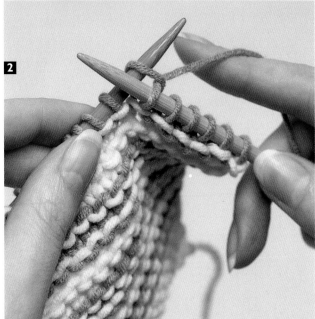

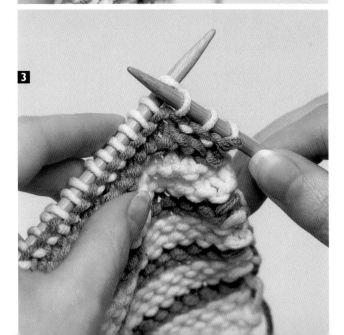

Striped garter-stitch cushion This tweedy little cushion has a modern country look, worked in toning yarns incorporating small flecks of colour. Tassels at each corner and wooden buttons add extra character. Colour changes on wrong-side rows create a mix of colours at the ends, while the central stripes have clear definition because the colours have been changed on right-side rows.

You will need

Pair of 4mm (no 8/US 6) knitting needles

2 x 50g (1¾oz) balls of wool/alpaca/viscose tweed yarn in red (A)

2 x 50g (1¾oz) balls wool/alpaca/viscose tweed yarn in pink (B)

Sewing needle and pins

3 buttons

26 x 45cm (10¼ x 18in) cushion pad

Tension

22 stitches and 38 rows over 10cm (4in) square of garter stitch

Finished size

26 x 45cm (10¼ x 18in)

Working the cushion cover front

Cast on 56 stitches using 4mm (no 8/US 6) needles and Yarn A.

Narrow stripes *1st row: Using Yarn A, K to end.

2nd and 3rd rows: Using Yarn B, K to end.

4th and 5th rows: Using Yarn A, K to end.

Rep 2nd to 5th rows 13 more times.

Wide stripes 1st to 9th rows: Using Yarn B, K to end.

10th and 11th rows: Using Yarn A, K to end.

12th to 19th rows: Using Yarn B, K to end *.

Rep 10th to 19th rows 4 more times.

Next row: Using Yarn B, K to end.

Narrow stripes 1st and 2nd rows: Using Yarn A, K to end.

3rd and 4th rows: Using Yarn B, K to end.

Rep 1st to 4th rows 13 more times.

Using Yarn A, cast off.

Working the cushion cover back

The cover back is worked in 2 pieces.

First piece Work as front from * to *.

Rep 10th to 19th rows once more.

Next row: Using Yarn A, K to end.

Using Yarn A, cast off.

Second piece Work as front from * to *.

Rep 10th to 19th rows twice more.

Next row: Using Yarn A, K to end.

Using Yarn A, cast off.

Making up the cushion cover

1 Press and block the front and back pieces to size. Lay out the front piece, right side up. Lay the first back piece (smaller) on top, right side down with the cast-on edge over the cast-on edge of the front piece.

2 Next, place the second back piece on top, right side down with the cast-on edge on the cast-off edge of the front piece, overlapping the 2 back pieces by 1 wide stripe in the centre. Pin and then backstitch the pieces together around all 4 edges, taking care to match the stripes, then turn the cover right sides out.

3 Work 3 loops (see page 145 for instructions) positioned evenly across the edge of the uppermost back piece and sew buttons on the piece beneath, to correspond with the loops.

4 Make 4 tassels (see page 146 for instructions) in Yarn A, each about 9cm (3½in) long.

5 Sew a tassel to each corner, insert the cushion pad and button the cover closed.

Striped stocking stitch

The two sides of a striped stocking-stitch fabric are quite different in appearance. On one side the stripes are edged with a clean line where the knit side of the stitch shows; on the other they are edged with a broken or dotted line where the purl side of the stitch shows. Although it is more usual to use the smooth side of the fabric with clean-edged stripes, the broken-edged stripe on the other side can also be used. It creates a more subtle transition between closely coloured stripes, or gives the appearance of two narrow stripes on either side of the join when the yarns are in highly contrasting shades.

Unlike garter stitch, which has the intersecting sides of the stitches alternating between the right and wrong sides of the fabric, stocking stitch has all the intersecting sides of the stitches on one side, which is usually used as the wrong side of the fabric.

Striped soft furnishings can be a resourceful way to use up oddments of yarn that are too small to knit a whole cushion cover. Choose yarns of a similar weight so that the tension is not affected too much. Wrap yarns around a piece of card to try out different colour combinations and stripe sequences before starting to knit.

1 Changing colours on either a right- or wrong-side row always creates a clean-edged colour change on the right side of the fabric. This happens because wrong-side rows are always purled.

2 On the wrong side of the fabric the colour change always has a broken edge.

3 By twisting the yarns at the end of a row, the yarn that is not in use can be carried up the selvedge without creating long strands. This makes a neater edge and helps to keep the final stitch before the colour change at the correct tension.

Pattern instructions

Yarns of different types or different colours are assigned a letter (Yarn A, Yarn B, etc.) or sometimes a number (Colour 1, Colour 2, etc.). The colour change for the stripe shown opposite would be written on a pattern as:

Yarn A: cream.

Yarn B: blue.

Using Yarn A

Work 4 rows st st starting with a K row.

Using Yarn B

Work 4 rows st st starting with a K row.

Always continue using the last stated yarn until told to change to a different one.

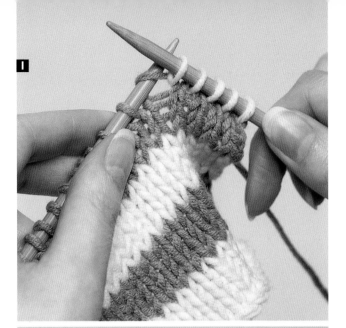

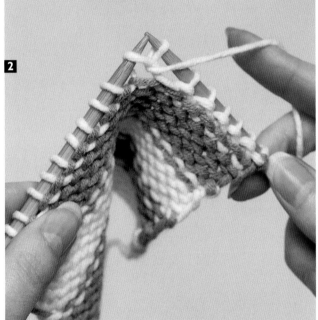

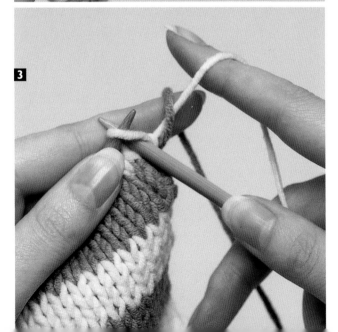

Striped bath mat This bath mat in navy and ecru is knitted in an unusual combination of cotton jersey strips and string to make it comfortable underfoot. Thick yarns, multiple strands and strips of other cotton fabrics could also be used to introduce different colours and textures. Knitting with rags tends to result in a firm, heavy fabric suitable for making a wide variety of rugs, sturdy bags and beach or picnic mats.

You will need

Pair of 10mm (no 000/
US 15) knitting needles

2 x 40m (44yds) balls of
medium-thickness cotton
string (A)

100cm (39½in) of 150cm
(59in) wide cotton jersey
fabric in ecru (B)

50cm (20in) of 150cm
(59in) wide cotton jersey
fabric in navy (C)

Dressmaker's scissors

Navy and ecru sewing
thread

Sewing needle and pins

Tension

8.5 stitches and 11 rows over
10cm (4in) square of st st

Finished size

50 x 78cm (20 x 30½in)

Cut the jersey into 2cm (⅞in) wide strips, across the width of the fabric. Each strip 150cm (59in) in length will knit a complete row.

Working the bath mat

With 10mm (no 000/US 15) needles and Yarn A, cast on 41 stitches.
The following 2 rows form stocking stitch.
1st row: K to end.
2nd row: P to end.
Rep these 2 rows as follows:
1st and 2nd rows: Using Yarn B.
3rd and 4th rows: Using Yarn A.
5th and 6th rows: Using Yarn B.
7th and 8th rows: Using Yarn C.
Rep these 8 rows, 9 more times.
Rep 1st to 6th rows once more.
Cast off in Yarn A.

Tie the ends of the strips together loosely at the beginning and end of each row as you knit to prevent unravelling.

Making up the bath mat

1 Untie the knotted strips at the beginning and end of each row. Trim then fold them back and backstitch them to the wrong side of the work with sewing thread in a matching colour to neaten the edges.
2 To complete the bath mat, press and block the piece to size. Work a fringe of string (Yarn A) along the cast-on and cast-off edges (see page 146 for instructions). For this you will need to cut 80 lengths of string, each 14cm (5½in) long.

Striped knit and purl stitches

Stripes can be combined with a number of stitches such as cables, slip stitch and knit-and-purl patterns. They can be colourful or tonal, cutting boldly across the stitch or helping to define certain areas of the stitch pattern. Once the effect that a stitch has on a stripe is understood, knitting patterns can be adapted to incorporate stripes for a different look or to enable you to use up leftover yarns. Small knit-and-purl patterns combined with narrow stripes are often used to create an all-over tweedy effect where the colours mix together and the pattern of knit and purl stitches is hardly visible. Wider stripes must be carefully placed so that they work within any changes of stitch.

1 Colour changes on a wide rib create strongly defined stripes within the knit areas and a more mixed effect within the purl areas, all within the same row. This is a 4 knit 4 purl rib with a stripe sequence of 2 rows of colour 1, 2 rows of colour 2.

2 The stripes on a narrow rib, such as this 1 knit 1 purl rib with a stripe sequence of 2 rows of colour 1, 2 rows of colour 2, look quite solid when the fabric is not stretched out, as the purl stitches are hidden. When the fabric is stretched horizontally, the stripe can appear to be wavy where it crosses the raised, vertical lines of knit stitches standing proud of the purl stitches.

3 When changing colours on a welt, the rules are just like those for garter stitch. Changing colour on a knitted right-side row or purled wrong-side row will create a clean-edged stripe (as on the second stripe up) whilst changing colour on a purled right-side row or knitted wrong-side row will create a broken-edged stripe (as on the bottom stripe).

Pattern instructions

Yarns of different types or different colours are assigned a letter (Yarn A, Yarn B, etc.) or sometimes a number (Colour 1, Colour 2, etc.). The colour change for a 2-colour, 2-row stripe on 4 x 4 rib as shown in 1 could be written on a pattern as:

Yarn A: cream
Yarn B: blue
Using Yarn A
1st row: K4, (P4, K4) to end.
2nd row: P4, (K4, P4) to end.
Using Yarn B
3rd row: K4, (P4, K4) to end.
4th row: P4, (K4, P4) to end.

Any more complicated knit-and-purl designs will be given in chart form, with one square representing one stitch as described on page 49. The squares will usually be shaded to reflect the colour changes, although black-and-white charts may instead use symbols with an explanatory key. You may find it useful to lightly shade the different areas with a pencil as symbols can be quite hard to follow.

Striped shoulder bag The relaxed style of this two-tone denim striped bag has all the character of your favourite pair of jeans. Use it as a shoulder bag or for stylish storage in the home. You could even customize your bag with fringing, beads or braid for a more elaborate look.

You will need

Pair of 4mm (no 8/US 6) knitting needles

Pair of 3mm (no 11/US 3) knitting needles

4 x 50g (1¾oz) balls of cotton yarn in dark denim (A)

1 x 50g (1¾oz) ball of cotton yarn in light denim (B)

Sewing needle and pins

1 metal button

Tension

Before washing: 20 stitches and 28 rows over 10cm (4in) square of P2, K6 rib

After washing: 20 stitches and 32 rows over 10cm (4in) square of P2, K6 rib

Finished size

21 x 30 x 5cm (8½ x 12 x 2in)

Working the shoulder bag front

With 4mm (no 8/US 6) needles and Yarn A, cast on 44 stitches.
1st row: K1, (P2, K6) to last 3 sts, P2, K1.
2nd row: P1, (K2, P6) to last 3 sts, K2, P1.
These 2 rows form a rib for the front and back.
Using Yarn A, work 24 rows of rib.
Stripes Using Yarn B, work 4 rows of rib.
Using Yarn A, work 4 rows of rib.
Using Yarn B, work 4 rows of rib.
Using Yarn A, work 4 rows of rib.
Using Yarn B, work 4 rows of rib.
Using Yarn A, work 48 rows of rib.
Cast off in rib.

Working the shoulder bag back and flap

Work as for the front, up to, but not including, the cast-off, then continue as follows:
Flap Using Yarn B, work 34 rows of rib.
1st buttonhole row: K1, (P2, K6) twice, P2, K2, cast off 2 sts, K2, (P2, K6) twice, P2, K1.
2nd buttonhole row: P1, (K2, P6) twice, K2, P2, cast on 2 sts, P2, (K2, P6) twice, K2, P1.
Work 2 more rows of rib.
Cast off in rib.

Working the strap, base and side section

These are all worked together in one long strip, starting in the centre of the base.
With 4mm (no 8/US 6) needles and Yarn A, cast on 12 stitches.

1st row: K1, P2, K6, P2, K1.
2nd row: P1, K2, P6, K2, P1.
These 2 rows form a rib for the sides and base.
First half of base: In Yarn A, work 37 rows of rib.
Corner row: K to end.
Side section Work 24 rows of rib.
Stripes Using Yarn B, work 4 rows of rib.
Using Yarn A, work 4 rows of rib.
Using Yarn B, work 4 rows of rib.
Using Yarn A, work 4 rows of rib.
Using Yarn B, work 4 rows of rib.
Using Yarn A, work 48 rows of rib.
Strap section Use 3mm (no 11/US 3) needles.
1st row: (K1, P1) to end.
Rep 1st row until the strap section measures at least 105cm (41½in), to finish up approximately 100cm (39½in) long after washing and ending with a wrong-side row. This is a suitable length for an adult, but adjust here if necessary.
Side section Use 4mm (no 8/US 6) needles.
1st row: K1, P2, K6, P2, K1.
2nd row: P1, K2, P6, K2, P1.
These 2 rows form a rib for the sides and the base.
Using Yarn A, work 48 rows of rib.
Stripes Using Yarn B, work 4 rows of rib.
Using Yarn A, work 4 rows of rib.
Using Yarn B, work 4 rows of rib.
Using Yarn A, work 4 rows of rib.
Using Yarn B, work 4 rows of rib.
Using Yarn A, work 24 rows of rib.

Corner row: P to end.
Work 37 rows of rib starting with a 2nd row.
Cast off in rib.

Making up the bag

1 Wash all the pieces in a washing machine at
a temperature of 60–70°C (140–160°F), so
that the correct amount of shrinkage can take
place. Block them out to size and leave to dry.
The front piece should measure 21 × 30cm
(8½ × 12in), the back piece 45 × 30cm
(18 × 12in) and the strip 5cm (2in) wide.
2 With right sides together, backstitch
the 2 ends of the strip together to form
a continuous loop. The rest of the bag is
sewn together with the seams showing
on the outside, using a small running stitch
(see page 142).
3 With wrong sides together, pin then stitch
the loop to the base and side sections of the
bag front. Match the seam in the loop to align
with the centre of the cast-on edge of the
front piece, match the purl rows to the corners
and the stripes to each other up the sides.
4 Repeat the process, stitching the other edge
of the loop to the back of the bag as far as the
light denim stripe that forms the bag flap.
5 Finish by sewing the button to the front
of the bag, aligning it with the buttonhole
on the flap, approximately 6cm (2½in)
from the top edge.

Circle-stripe cushion This pattern of circles within stripes is clearly defined when worked in a smooth, regular yarn such as this wool/cotton blend. You can adapt the design to make a fabulous matching throw in a single colour. Work six design repeats across the width and repeat the whole chart twice lengthways; this would require 12 50g (1¾oz) balls of yarn. Finish the edges with ribbon, mitred at the corners.

You will need

Pair of 4mm (no 8/US 6) knitting needles

Pair of 3.25mm (no 10/ US 4) knitting needles

4 x 50g (1¾oz) balls of cotton/wool yarn in pale green (A)

2 x 50g (1¾oz) balls of cotton/wool yarn in violet (B)

Sewing needle and pins

3 buttons

45cm (18in) square cushion pad

Tension

22 stitches and 30 rows over 10cm (4in) square of patterned fabric

Finished size

45cm (18in) square

Working the cushion cover front

With 4mm (no 8/US 6) needles and Yarn A, cast on 100 stitches.
Work all 138 rows of the design (see chart on page 155). Cast off in Yarn A.

Working the cushion cover back

First piece With 4mm (no 8/US 6) needles and Yarn A, cast on 100 stitches.
First stripe: Using Yarn A, work 24 rows of rev st st, starting with a P row.
Second stripe: Using Yarn B, work 23 rows of st st, starting and finishing with a K row.
Third stripe: Using Yarn A, P 1 row then work 17 rows of rev st st, starting with a P row.
Button band Use 3.25mm (no 10/US 4) needles. Using Yarn A
1st row: K1 (P2, K2) to last 3 sts, P2, K1.
2nd row: P1 (K2, P2) to last 3 sts, K2, P1.
Rep 1st and 2nd rows once more.
1st buttonhole row: K1 (P2, K2) 6 times, *cast off 2 sts, K2, (P2, K2) 5 times *, rep from * to * twice more, P2, K1.
2nd buttonhole row: P1 (K2, P2) 6 times, *cast on 2 sts, P2, (K2, P2) 5 times *, rep from * to * twice more, K2, P1.
Rep 1st and 2nd rows of button band (without buttonholes) twice more.
Cast off in rib.

Second piece With 3.25mm (no 10/US 4) needles and Yarn A, cast on 100 stitches.
Button band Using Yarn A
1st row: P1, (K2, P2) to last 3 sts, K2, P1.
2nd row: K1, (P2, K2) to last 3 sts, P2, K1.
Rep 1st and 2nd rows 4 more times.
Change to 4mm (no 8/US 6) needles.
First stripe: Using Yarn A, work 16 rows of st st, starting with a K row.
Second stripe: Using Yarn B, K 1 row then work 24 rows of rev st st, starting with a K row.
Third stripe: Using Yarn A, work 24 rows of st st starting with a P row.
Cast off purlwise.

Making up the cushion cover

1 Press and block the front and back pieces to size. Lay out the front piece, right side up. Lay the first back piece on top, right side down, with the cast-on edge over the edge of the front.
2 Place the second back piece on top, right side down, with the cast-off edge over the cast-off edge of the front piece, overlapping the button bands in the centre. Pin then backstitch the pieces together around all 4 edges, taking care to match the stripes.
3 Turn the cover right sides out and sew buttons on the button band underneath. Insert the cushion pad and button closed.

Cables

Cables create a richly textured surface, with a more pronounced effect than knit-and-purl patterns. Instead of being worked in the same order as they come off the needle, the stitches are moved from one position to another in the same row, resulting in crossovers that build into a plaited, rope-like pattern. To construct a cable, a number of stitches are slipped from the knitting needle onto one end of a cable needle, where they are held while the next few stitches are knitted as normal. The held stitches are then knitted off the other end of the cable needle in the same order as they came off the knitting needle. A number of normal rows are then worked between crossovers. Cables are usually worked on stocking stitch with the stitches on either side in reverse stocking stitch, as this utilizes the tendency for ribs to throw the cabled areas into relief. The stitches that cross are stretched and slope diagonally across the fabric, pulling it in dramatically widthways and slightly lengthways. The more frequent the cables, the thicker and firmer is the fabric.

Use a cable needle in a slightly smaller size than the needles you are knitting with. Pull the yarn firmly when knitting the first stitch from the left needle while stitches are being held on the cable needle to avoid gaps in the fabric. Use a row marker to help count the rows between crossovers.

Back-cross cable

On this type of cable, also known as right-cross cable, the stitches that are held lie across the back of the fabric and those that are knitted first are seen on the face. This results in a cable that slopes from bottom left to top right. They can be worked singly or in formation to make more complex designs. The number of rows between cables can also be varied and it is usual to leave larger gaps between cables worked over a greater number of stitches. Cables are usually balanced, with an even number of stitches divided equally for crossing, although asymmetrical cables are possible. If only two stitches are being crossed, a cable needle is not required, but the miniature cable formed does not have the depth of wider cables.

Here the cable is being worked over 4 stitches with reverse stocking stitch at either side, but the principle is the same for any number of stitches. The greater the number of stitches that are crossed and the heavier the yarn, the more pronounced will be the texture of the pattern.

1 On a right-side row work up to the rib, then slip the next 2 stitches on to a cable needle.
2 With the stitches on the cable needle held at the back of the work, knit the 2 stitches from the left needle.
3 Knit the 2 stitches from the cable needle in their original order to make a crossover.
4 Continue working the row as normal. A number of rows will then be worked following the same knit and purl sequence but without a crossover.

Pattern instructions
A back-cross cable over 4 stitches would be written on a pattern as 'C4B', over 6 stitches as 'C6B', etc. A cable stitch can also be shown as a symbol on a chart, particularly when combined with knit and purl stitch patterns. A bottom left to top right sloping diagonal line across the appropriate number of squares, is then used to represent a back-cross cable.

Count the rows between the cables carefully as you knit. The distortion caused by the crossings can make it quite difficult to count them afterwards.

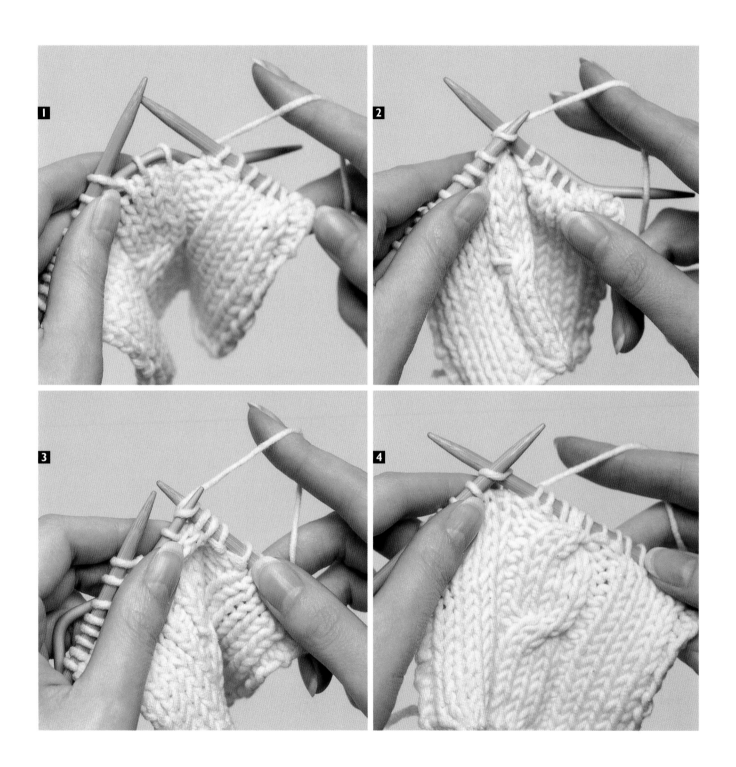

Cabled bolster cushion

This is the simplest of knitted cable structures, with all the crosses positioned at regular intervals and in the same direction. Worked in plush, velvety chenille yarn, it makes a luxurious cover for a bolster cushion, especially when finished at each end with these chunky, tasselled cord ties.

You will need

Pair of 5mm (no 6/US 8) knitting needles

Cable needle

4 x 100g (3½oz) hanks of chunky cotton chenille yarn in ecru

Sewing thread

Sewing needle and pins

45cm long x 17cm diameter (18 x 7in) bolster cushion inner

Tension

14 stitches and 23 rows over 10cm (4in) square of st st

Finished fabric when flat

88 x 60cm (34½ x 23½in)

Working the bolster cover

With 5mm (no 6/US 8) needles, cast on a total of 86 stitches.

End section Work 42 rows of st st, starting with a K row.

Next row: P to end.

Cabled section *1st row (wrong-side row): K2, (P4, K2) to end.

2nd row: P2, (K4, P2) to end.

3rd row: K2, (P4, K2) to end.

Rep 2nd and 3rd rows once more.

6th row: P2, (K4, P2, C4B, P2) to end *.

These 6 rows, from * to *, form cable patt.

Rep cable patt 15 more times.

Rep 1st to 5th rows once more.

End section Next row: P to end.

Work 42 rows of st st, starting with a P row.

Cast off purlwise.

Avoid twisting the yarn as you knit, as this can crush the pile. Chenille has very little give so it needs to be worked quite firmly, but not so that it breaks when the fabric is stretched.

Making up the cover

1 Press and block the piece to size. Fold it in half along its length, with right sides together, then pin and backstitch the 2 edges in a seam along the entire length, matching knitting stitch to knitting stitch to create a tube.

2 Turn the cover right side out. Make 2 cords, each requiring about 10 strands of yarn 150cm (59in) long to make a cord 60cm (23½in) long when finished (see page 148 for instructions on making cords). Tie the ends of both pieces of cord in a knot 6cm (2½in) from the end, then trim and untwist the loose strands to create a tassel effect.

3 To complete the bolster, slip the cushion inside the tube of knitting and position it within the cabled section between the 2 purl rows. Gather and tie the fabric at the ends with the cords.

Front-cross cable

On this type of cable the stitches that are held are seen on the front of the fabric and the stitches that are knitted first lie across the back. This results in a cable that slopes from bottom right to top left.

Once the basic principles of working a cable are understood, creating all manner of cable designs is just a matter of careful counting. Repeating the same type of cable produces a rope-like appearance, but by alternating between front and back crosses a wavy cable (sometimes called a ribbon cable) is created. Two crosses can be worked side by side, with no reverse stocking stitch between; for example, a front and back cross side by side make a staghorn cable but if they are staggered a plait cable results. These patterns will be familiar because of the heavily textured sweaters, originally worn by fishermen, traditionally knitted on the isles of Guernsey and Aran.

Cables also combine well with knit and purl stitches, the most basic example being alternating plain ribs with cables separated by reverse stocking stitch. As an alternative to reverse stocking stitch, garter stitch creates more pronounced ridges that contrast well with the cables or use moss stitch for added texture. Cables can be incorporated in all sorts of single and multicolour designs.

The cable in the example shown is being worked over 4 stitches with two reverse stocking stitches at either side; the principle is the same for any number of stitches. Front-cross cables are sometimes referred to as left-cross cables.

1 On a right-side row work right up to the rib, then slip the next 2 stitches onto a cable needle.

2 With the stitches on the cable needle held at the front of the work, knit the 2 stitches from the left needle.

3 Now knit the 2 stitches from the cable needle in their original order in order to make a crossover.

4 Continue working the row as normal. A number of rows will then be worked following the same knit and purl sequence but without a crossover.

Pattern instructions

A front-cross cable over 4 stitches would be written on a pattern as 'C4F', over 6 stitches as 'C6F', etc. A cable stitch is also shown as a symbol on a chart, particularly useful when combined with knit and purl stitches. A bottom right to top left sloping diagonal line across the appropriate number of squares is then used to represent a front- cross cable.

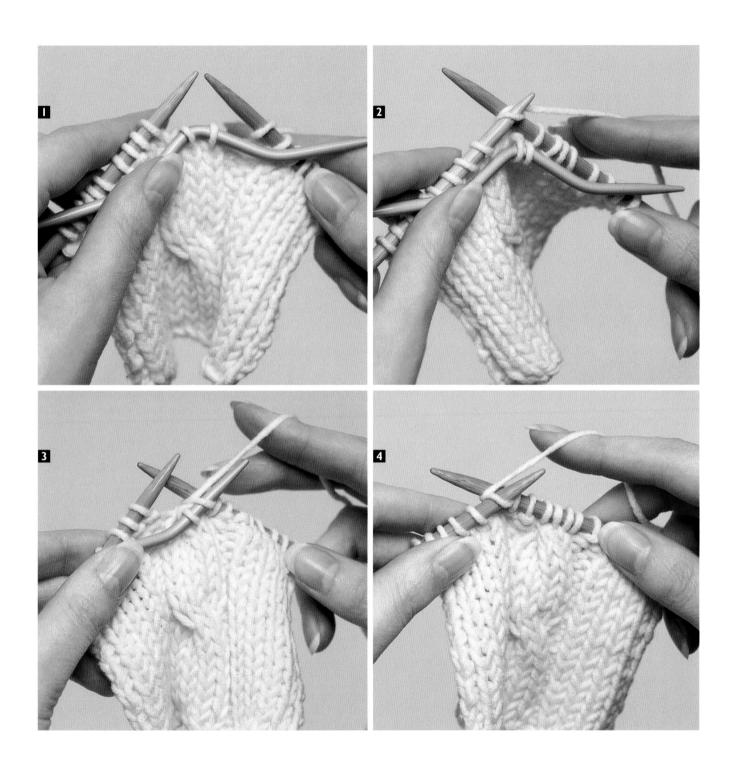

Pillar cable cushion The lovely mix of hand-dyed colours together with the chunky, irregular nature of the yarn give a rugged character to this cushion cover. Heavy, staghorn cables are created by working a front-cross and a back-cross cable side by side. The ribs are reminiscent of pillars, with the cables as decorative carvings at the top. These are set against a cover back worked in reverse stocking stitch.

You will need

Pair of 6mm (no 4/US 10) knitting needles

Pair of 5mm (no 6/US 8) knitting needles

Cable needle

5 x 100g (3½oz) hanks of wool/cotton twist yarn in moss

Sewing needle and pins

4 buttons

50cm (20in) square cushion pad

Tension

13½ stitches and 20 rows over 10cm (4in) square of st st

Finished size

50cm (20in) square

Working the cushion cover front

With 6mm (no 4/US 10) needles, cast on a total of 68 stitches.

Rib section 1st row: P2, (K12, P1) 5 times, P1.
2nd row: K2, (P12, K1) 5 times, K1.
Rep 1st and 2nd rows 25 more times.

First cable section 1st row: P2, (C6B, C6F, P1, K12, P1) twice, C6B, C6F, P2.
2nd row: K2, (P12, K1) 5 times, K1.
3rd row: P2, (K12, P1) 5 times, P1.
4th row: Rep 2nd row.
5th row: Rep 3rd row.
6th row: Rep 2nd row.
Rep 1st to 6th rows twice more.

Second cable section 1st row: P15, C6B, C6F, P14, C6B, C6F, P15.
2nd row: K15, P12, K14, P12, K15.
3rd row: P15, K12, P14, K12, P15.
4th row: Rep 2nd row.
5th row: Rep 3rd row.
6th row: Rep 2nd row.
Rep 1st to 6th rows twice more.

Top section Work 12 rows of rev st st, starting with a P row.
Cast off purlwise.

Working the cushion cover back

The back is knitted in 2 pieces.

First piece With 6mm (no 4/US 10) needles, cast on 68 stitches.

Work 46 rows of rev st st, starting with a P row.

Button band Change to 5mm (no 6/US 8) needles. (See page 145 for instructions for eyelet buttonholes.)

1st row: (P1, K1) to end.

Rep 1st row once more.

Buttonhole row: (P1, K1) 7 times, Yfwd, K2tog, P1, (K1, P1) 5 times, Yrn, P2tog, K1, (P1, K1) 5 times, Yfwd, K2tog, P1, (K1, P1) 5 times, Yrn, P2tog, (K1, P1) to last stitch, K1.

Rep 1st row of button band twice more.

Cast off in rib.

Second piece With 5mm (no 6/US 8) needles, cast on 68 stitches.

Button band 1st row: (P1, K1) to end.

Rep 1st row 4 more times.

Change to 6mm (no 4/US 10) needles.

Work 46 rows of rev st st, starting with a K row.

Cast off.

Making up the cushion cover

1 Press and block the front and back pieces to size. Lay out the front piece, right side up. Lay the first back piece (with buttonholes) on top, reverse stocking-stitch side down, and with the cast-on edge over the cast-on edge of the front piece.

2 Next, place the second back piece on top, reverse stocking-stitch side down, with the cast-off edge over the cast-off edge of the front piece, so that the button bands overlap in the centre. Pin, then backstitch the pieces together around all 4 edges.

3 Turn the cover right sides out and sew buttons on the button band underneath to correspond with the buttonholes. Insert the cushion pad and button the cover closed.

Cabled heart hot-water-bottle cover Cuddle up to this blissfully soft and fluffy hot-water bottle cover. Knitted in rosy pink angora wool, which is wonderfully soft to the touch, and with a big heart design, it is unashamedly feminine. There are no shapings to worry about, as this cover is simply gathered at the top with a drawstring, creating a lovely ruffled effect. This design would also make a pretty drawstring storage bag.

You will need

Pair of 4.5mm (no 7/US 7) knitting needles

Cable needle

1 x 80g (2¾oz) ball of angora/lambswool yarn in pink

Sewing needle and pins

33 x 20cm (13 x 8in) hot-water bottle

Tension

21 stitches and 28 rows over 10cm (4in) square of st st

Finished size

36 x 22cm (14 x 8½in)

Working the hot-water bottle cover front

With 4.5mm (no 7/US 7) needles, cast on 49 stitches.

Below heart Work 18 rows of st st, starting with a K row.

Heart motif Work the next 38 rows from the chart on page 155, with 12 stitches of st st on either side of the motif.

Above heart Work 28 rows of st st, starting with a K row.

Eyelet row K3, (Yfwd, K2tog, K4) 7 times, Yfwd, K2tog, K2. (See page 145 for instructions for working eyelets.)

Top ruffle Work 15 rows of st st, starting and finishing with a P row.

Work 2 rows of rev st st, starting with a P row.

Work 4 rows of st st, starting with a K row. Cast off.

Working the hot-water bottle cover back

Work a second piece in exactly the same way as the cover front.

Making up the cover

1 Handwash both pieces gently in warm water, taking care not to rub or ring. After a short spin in a pillowcase, block the pieces to size and leave to dry naturally. With right sides together, pin and then backstitch the pieces together around 3 of the sides, leaving the ruffle end open.

2 Make a cord 55cm (22in) long, for which you will need 6 strands of yarn each 200cm (79in) long (see page 148 for instructions).

3 Turn the cover right sides out and thread the cord in and out of the eyelet holes, starting and finishing in the middle of the front.

4 To complete the hot-water bottle cover, insert the hot-water bottle, then tie the ends of the cord together in a bow, gathering up the fabric to close the cover.

Multicolour
Pattern

There are a number of knitting techniques that allow multicolour designs to break out of the orderly constraints of straight-edged stripes. Different techniques are suited to different designs, depending on the number of colours used and the size of the areas of colour. The pattern instructions will usually state the most appropriate technique. Different traditions in colour knitting have grown up around the world and it is fascinating to see how the technique and the commonly worked designs go hand in hand.

Simple patterns can be created by combining elongated slip stitches with coloured stripes, with only one yarn used at a time. All-over, blocky, slip-stitch patterns are sometimes called 'mosaic knitting'. Where more than one yarn is used within a row, the possibilities for colourful figurative and geometric designs really open up. Fair Isle is a term used for colour knitting where the colours not showing on the face of the fabric lie across the back. The name refers to the tiny island of Fair Isle between The Orkneys and The Shetlands of the coast of Scotland, believed to be the birthplace of the technique. There is also a strong tradition for this type of knitting in Scandinavia and South America. Intarsia knitting involves working areas with separate balls of yarn, which must be crossed at the edges to join the different areas together. The name intarsia comes from the Arabic word for mosaic.

Slip patterns

Slipping a stitch means simply transferring it from one needle to another without working it. The slip method can be combined with coloured stripes to make a fabric appear to have been knitted with two colours in a row, whereas in fact only a single colour is worked at any one time. This makes a piece almost as straightforward to knit as a simple stripe. When slipped consecutively for more than one row, the elongated stitch drags the colour from one row up into subsequent rows and this also gives the fabric added texture. In addition, the slip method can be used to construct textured knits in a single colour. This is because the tension caused by the elongated stitches can distort the knitted fabric, creating raised and recessed areas or long and short stitches.

Checks, stripes, zigzags and diamonds are common multicolour slip patterns. For colourwork the yarn is usually held at the back to show just the held stitch on the face of the fabric. Sometimes the yarn might be required to be held at the front if a horizontal bar is required (for example, with bead knitting described on pages 132–3). Fabrics with a lot of slipped stitches can be slow to grow.

A strand of the yarn that is being worked is carried across the back of the slipped stitches and forms a float. Stitches are simplest to slip purlwise, as it is not necessary to change the direction in which the needle is inserted from the usual position. In the design opposite, 2 stitches are worked then 2 stitches are slipped, repeating across the fabric for the 2 rows worked in blue.

On a knit row

1 To slip a stitch on a knit row, with the yarn away from you on the wrong side of the work, insert the right needle into the front of the stitch as if you were going to purl. This will prevent the stitch from being twisted. Without passing the yarn around the needle, drop the stitch from the left needle to the right. When the next stitch is knitted following the design, take care not to pull the yarn too tightly.

On a purl row

2 To slip a stitch on a purl row, with the yarn facing you on the wrong side of the work, insert the right needle into the front of the stitch as if you were going to purl. Without passing the yarn around the needle, drop the stitch from the left needle to the right. When the next stitch is purled following the design, take care not to pull the yarn too tightly.

Pattern instructions

A slip stitch would be written on a pattern as 'sl', followed by the number of stitches to be slipped, eg 'sl1', 'sl2', etc. Leave the yarn where it is, unless the instructions state 'wyif' (with yarn in front) or 'wyab' (with yarn at back). A slip pattern could also be given in chart form with a symbol such as a 'v' representing a slipped stitch.

On a knit row

1

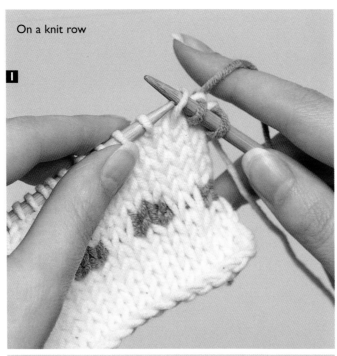

On a purl row

2

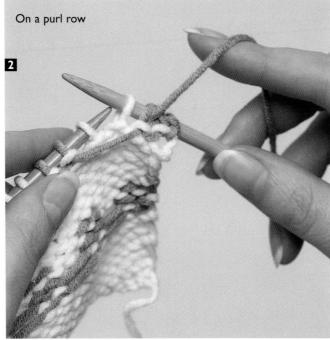

Contrast-block cushion Big blocks of colour in soft, neutral tones allow the natural beauty of this hairy mohair yarn to come into its own. Small, geometric slip-stitch details link the two colours together while coconut-shell buttons continue the theme of natural colour and texture.

You will need

Pair of 5mm (no 6/US 8) knitting needles

2 x 50g (1¾oz) balls of lambswool/mohair yarn in cream (A)

3 x 50g (1¾oz) balls of lambswool/mohair yarn in beige (B)

Sewing thread, needle and pins

5 buttons

50cm (20in) square cushion pad

Tension

19 stitches and 25 rows over 10cm (4in) square of st st

Finished size

50cm (20in) square

Working the cushion cover front

With 5mm (no 6/US 8) needles and Yarn A, cast on 97 stitches.

* Work 30 rows of st st, starting with a K row.

First slip-stitch band Using Yarn B

1st row: K4, (sl1, K3) to last stitch, K1.

2nd row: P4, (sl1, P3) to last stitch, P1.

Using Yarn A

Work 30 rows of st st, starting with a K row.

Second slip-stitch band Using Yarn B

1st row: K2, (sl1, K1) to last stitch, K1.

2nd row: P2, (sl1, P1) to last stitch, P1 *.

Using Yarn B

Work 30 rows of st st, starting with a K row.

Third slip-stitch band **Using Yarn A

1st row: K4, (sl1, K3) to last stitch, K1.

2nd row: P4, (sl1, P3) to last stitch, P1.

Using Yarn B

Work 30 rows of st st, starting with a K row.

Cast off **.

Working the cushion cover back

The cover back (shown here) is knitted in 2 pieces.

First piece With 5mm (no 6/US 8) needles and Yarn B, cast on 97 stitches.

Work 4 rows of st st, starting with a K row.

Buttonhole row: K16, (yfwd, K2tog, K14) 4 times, yfwd, K2tog, K15.

(See pages 143–5 for instructions for working eyelet buttonholes.)

Work 5 rows of st st, starting and finishing with a P row.

Turning row: P to end.

Work 5 rows of st st, starting and finishing with a P row.

Buttonhole row: K16, (yfwd, K2 tog, K14) 4 times, yfwd, K2 tog, K15.

Work 15 rows of st st, starting and finishing with a P row.

Continue as for the front, from ** to **.

Second piece With 5mm (no 6/US 8) needles and Yarn A, cast on 97 stitches.

Work as for the front from * to *.

Work 19 rows of st st, starting and ending with a K row.

Turning row: K to end.

Work 10 rows of st st, starting with a K row.

Cast off.

Making up the cushion cover

1 Press and block the front and back pieces to size. Finish the button edges of the 2 back pieces by folding them back from the raised line of purl stitches and sewing in place. The 2 rows of eyelet holes on the first piece should be aligned so that the buttons can pass through both layers.

2 Lay out the front piece, right side up. Place the first back piece (with eyelet holes) on top, right side down, with the cast-off edge over the cast-off edge of the front piece.

3 Next, lay the second back piece on top, right side down, with the cast-on edge over the cast-on edge of the front piece, creating an overlap in the middle. Pin then backstitch the pieces together around all 4 edges, taking care to match the stripes.

4 Turn the cover right sides out and sew buttons on the back piece underneath to correspond with the buttonholes. Insert the cushion pad and button the cover closed.

Fair Isle – stranding colours

Fair Isle knitting (sometimes also called jacquard) is a little trickier to work than slip stitch because two or more colours are worked in the same row and both are carried the full width of the piece. To achieve this, two or more yarns must be held in the hand at the same time so that they can be worked when required. Carrying yarn across the back of the fabric can make it look and feel quite different from the plain stocking-stitch equivalent. The stitch size tends to be slightly bigger, the fabrics are less elastic because the floats (see below) tend to hold them in widthways, and they use more yarn and consequently are heavier in weight.

Stranded Fair Isle is usually worked in stocking stitch and is an ideal technique for small, regular patterns that have two colours in the row and where the colours alternate every few stitches. Snowflakes, O and X designs, and striped two- and three-row motifs called 'peerie' (meaning small in Shetland dialect) designs are some of the traditional patterns for this technique. One or both of the colours can be changed at the beginning of a new row, making colourful striped patterns, incorporating a number of colours, although generally only two at a time. More can be worked simultaneously but the range of pattern possibilities is severely restricted by the size of the float.

Where colours are stranded, the colour that is not being worked is just carried across the back of the row until it is needed, and this strand of yarn is called a float. The maximum practical length for a float is 2–3cm (1in), or sometimes a maximum of four consecutive stitches of the same colour is used as a guide. It is easier to control the tension of shorter floats and they are less likely to be snagged when the finished article is in use. Floats that are too tight will stop the fabric from lying flat, so make them loose enough to allow the fabric to stretch a little.

There are many different ways in which the yarns can be held while working stranded Fair Isle, but the resulting fabric is the same no matter which method is used. The yarn can be picked up while being worked and then dropped and the other yarn picked up, but this is a slow process. One yarn could be held in the left hand and one in the right, both could be held in the left hand or, as shown opposite, both in the right hand.

Hold the main colour over the index finger and the second colour over the middle finger.

On knit rows

1 Knit up to the colour change with the main colour, while carrying the second colour loosely across the wrong side of the work. Always bring the main colour in above the contrast colour.

2 In order to knit a stitch in the second colour, insert the needle in the next stitch and pass the second colour around the tip (this will involve turning the hand very slightly) and draw the colour through. Always bring the contrast colour in below the main colour.

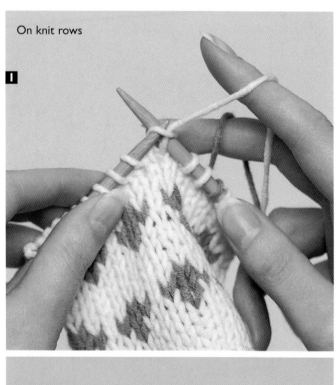

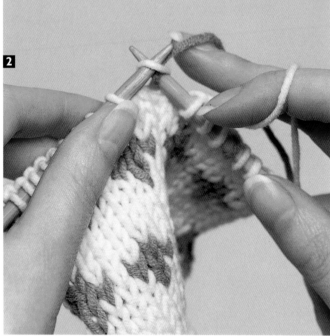

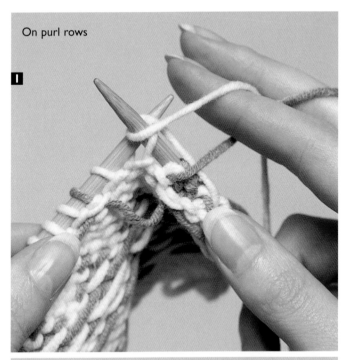

On purl rows

1

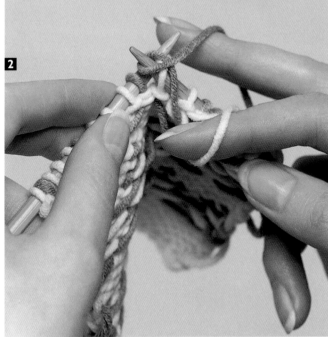

2

On purl rows

1 Purl right up to the colour change with the main colour, while carrying the second colour loosely across the wrong side of the work which is now visible as you knit. Always bring the main colour in above the contrast colour.

2 In order to purl a stitch in the second colour, insert the needle in the next stitch and then pass the second colour around the tip and draw the colour through. Always bring the contrast colour in below the main colour.

Stranding in the same order ensures that the same colour always lies on top; this has a neater appearance from the back and ensures that the stitches in a row look uniform on the front of the fabric. Keep the stitches spread on the needle as you knit so that the float will not be pulled too tightly.

Pattern instructions

Instructions for Fair Isle are usually given as a chart. The pattern is shown on a squared grid where one square represents one stitch. It is read in the same way as you knit. The bottom row of the chart, representing the first row of knitting, should be read from right to left, and the second row from left to right – this continues as you move up the chart.

For a stocking-stitch fabric, the first row would be knit and the second row would be purl. Colours are represented by symbols, or alternatively the squares are shaded in the appropriate colour. With a

repeating pattern, where the motif repeats right across the piece, then often only one full repeat will be shown. This will be marked with a heavy outline and an indication that it is to be repeated. There may also be extra stitches on either side that are incomplete motifs, added to balance the design within the knitted piece. The number of times the rows are to be repeated may be marked on the chart or given in the instructions.

Reading the chart in this way, count and then knit the number of stitches in the first colour. Count and then knit the number of stitches in the second colour. Continue counting and changing colours all along the row. Once the pattern is established, it becomes easier because you can continue in the same rhythm and just glance at the chart to see how the pattern has changed from the previous row. Put a marker above the row you are working so that you do not lose your place but can also see how the current row relates to previous ones.

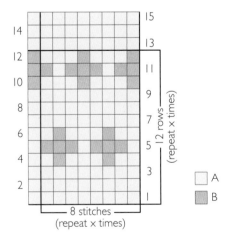

Fair Isle band cushion Butterflies and flowers in black, brown and cream have a charming retro look. The intricately patterned band is set against a plain background, highlighting the detail and making it quicker and easier to knit than an all-over design.

You will need

Pair of 4mm (no 8/US 6) knitting needles

Pair of 3mm (no 11/US 3) knitting needles

3 x 50g (1¾oz) balls of dk merino wool yarn in white (A)

1 x 50g (1¾oz) ball of dk merino wool yarn in black (B)

1 x 50g (1¾oz) ball of dk merino wool yarn in brown (C)

Sewing needle and pins

3 buttons

45cm (18in) square cushion pad

Tension

22 stitches and 30 rows over 10cm (4in) square of st st

22 stitches and 24 rows over 10cm (4in) square of Fair Isle

Finished size

45cm (18in) square

Working the cushion cover front

With 4mm (no 8/US 6) needles and Yarn A, cast on 101 stitches.
Using Yarn A, work 46 rows of st st, starting with a K row.
Fair Isle band Work the 42-row repeat of the design once using Yarns A–C (see chart on page 156) in st st, starting with a K row.
In Yarn A, work 46 rows of st st, starting with a K row. Cast off in Yarn A.

Working the cushion cover back

First piece With 3mm (no 11/US 3) needles and Yarn A, cast on 101 stitches.
Button band 1st row: K1, (P1, K1) to end.
2nd row: P1, (K1, P1) to end.
Rep 1st and 2nd rows once more.
1st buttonhole row: K1, (P1, K1) 11 times, * cast off 3 sts, K1, (P1, K1) 11 times, rep from * to end.
2nd buttonhole row: P1, (K1, P1) 11 times, *cast on 3 sts, P1, (K1, P1) 11 times, rep from * to end.
Rep 1st and 2nd button-band rows (without buttonholes) twice more.
With 4mm (no 8/US 6) needles and using Yarn A, work 8 rows of st st, starting with a K row.
Work the first 10 rows of the Fair Isle band (see chart) in st st, starting with a K row.
Using Yarn A, work 46 rows of st st, starting with a K row. Cast off in Yarn A.

Second piece With 4mm (no 8/US 6) needles and Yarn A, cast on 101 stitches.
Using Yarn A, work 46 rows of st st, starting with a K row.
Work the first 10 rows of the Fair Isle band, as shown on the chart, in st st, starting with a K row.
Using Yarn A, work 8 rows of st st, starting with a K row.
Button band Use 3mm (no 11/US 3) needles.
1st row: K1, (P1, K1) to end.
2nd row: P1, (K1, P1) to end.
Rep 1st and 2nd rows 4 more times.
Cast off in rib.

Making up the cushion cover

1 Press and block the front and back pieces. Lay out the cover front, right side up. Lay the first back piece (with buttonholes) on top, right side down, with the cast-off edge over the cast-off edge of the front.
2 Place the second back piece on top, right side down, with the cast-on edge over the cast-on edge of the front, overlapping the central button bands. Pin then backstitch the pieces together around all four edges, taking care to match the Fair Isle stripes.
3 Turn the cover right sides out and sew buttons on the button band underneath, to match the buttonholes. Insert the cushion pad and button the cover closed.

Woven-in Fair Isle

Where colours are woven in, the colour that is not being worked is woven over and under the stitches on the wrong side of the fabric. Designs are no longer restricted by the length of floats, which enables a wider range of pattern possibilities with larger areas of solid colour and unbroken shapes to be knitted. Woven-in Fair Isle is more difficult to knit than stranded because of the extra movement required to catch the yarn in and the extra concentration involved in doing so. The two techniques can be combined in different areas of a design according to the requirements of the design but care must be taken to match the tensions of the two techniques.

Weaving in the floating yarns is not necessary on every stitch – in fact, this can cause the stitches to become irregular, the yarns to show through at the front and an inflexible fabric to develop. Weave in on every third or fourth stitch but try to weave in on a different stitch on every row to prevent a vertical ridge forming. With experience you will be able to look at the design and anticipate the best places to weave in the float yarn. The size of the floats will be restricted to a similar length as on a stranded Fair Isle, but the resulting fabric is thicker and more stable.

Weaving in colours

Yarns can be held in the right hand, left hand, one in each or, if using more than two yarns, a combination of both. Depending on the way in which the yarns are held, which is being worked and which is floating, there are techniques for achieving the same structure, some of which involve awkward manoeuvres.

Working with three yarns is an added complication. To make it easier, treat both of the yarns not being worked as one and whenever one yarn needs to be woven in, weave in both. By doing this you are less likely to leave one behind.

Work the colours in the same way as stranded Fair Isle until you reach a point where it is necessary to weave in the float. The basic principle of weaving in is most clearly shown and easiest to knit when the working yarn is in the right hand and the floating yarn in the

left. If you have difficulty working colours from the left hand, you might find it easiest to swap yarns as you go along so that the working yarn is always held in the right hand.

On knit rows

1 On knit rows, bring up the float, insert the needle in the stitch, under the float, and knit the new stitch as usual, drawing it under the float. This leaves the float between the working yarn and the new stitch. When the next stitch in the row is knitted above the float, the float is caught in the back of the stitch. This is not visible from the right side of the work.

On purl rows

2 The same applies to purl rows. The stitch is purled under the float and when the next stitch in the row is purled above the float, the float is caught in the back of the stitch. This is clearly visible on the wrong side of the fabric, which is facing you.

Pattern instructions

Instructions for Fair Isle are usually given in the form of a chart as explained on page 99.

This technique can be used to weave in the ends created by the introduction of a new yarn at the beginning of a row on a striped fabric. Weave the ends of the old and new yarns alternately under and over the first few stitches of the new yarn, on the back of the fabric.

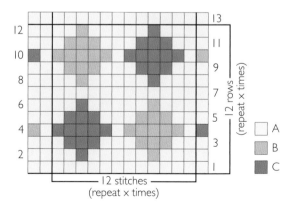

On knit rows

1

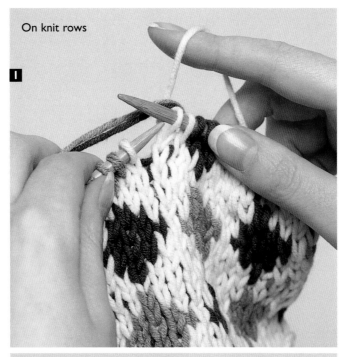

On purl rows

2

Leaf cushion This three-colour, geometric design is time-consuming to knit but the effort is amply rewarded. The pattern of the cover front is set against a plain back and framed with an edging of hand-twisted cord. To make working in two yarns easier, treat them as one and weave in both – you are less likely to leave one behind.

You will need

Pair of 4mm (no 8/US 6) knitting needles

Pair of 3.25mm (no 10/US 4) knitting needles

4 x 50g (1¾oz) balls of wool/cotton yarn in cream (A)

2 x 50g (1¾oz) balls of wool/cotton yarn in violet (B)

1 x 50g (1¾oz) balls of wool/cotton yarn in beige (C)

Sewing needle and pins

5 buttons

41cm (16in) square cushion pad

Tension

Front: 24 stitches and 20 rows over 10cm (4in) square of woven-in Fair Isle knitting

Back: 22 stitches and 30 rows over 10cm (4in) square of st st

Finished size

41cm (16in) square

Working the cushion cover front

With 4mm (no 8/US 6) needles and Yarn A, cast on 99 stitches.
Work 81 rows of the design (as indicated on the chart on page 156) in st st, using Yarns A–C and starting with a K row. Weave in yarns on every 3rd or 4th stitch.
Using Yarn A, cast off purlwise.

Working the cushion cover back

The back is worked in 2 pieces.
First piece With 4mm (no 8/US 6) needles and Yarn A, cast on 89 stitches.
Work 57 rows of st st, starting with a K row.
Change to 3.25mm (no 10/US 4) needles.
Button band (starting with a wrong-side row)
1st row: K1, (P1, K1) to end.
2nd row: P1, (K1, P1) to end.
Rep 1st and 2nd rows once, then repeat 1st row once more.
Buttonhole row: (P1, K1) 8 times, *Yfwd, K2tog, (P1, K1) 6 times *, rep from * to * 4 more times, P1, K1, P1.
Rep 1st and 2nd rows twice, then repeat 1st row once more.
Cast off in rib.
Second piece With 3.25mm (no 10/US 4) needles and Yarn A, cast on 89 stitches.
Button band 1st row: P1, (K1, P1) to end.
2nd row: K1, (P1, K1) to end.

Rep 1st and 2nd rows 4 more times, then repeat 1st row once more.
Change to 4mm (no 8/US 6) needles.
Work 57 rows of st st, starting with a P row.
Cast off.

Making up the cushion cover

1 Press and block the front and back pieces to size. Lay out the front piece, right side up. Lay the first back piece (with buttonholes) on top, with the cast-on edge over the cast-on edge of the front piece.
2 Place the second back piece on top, with the cast-off edge placed directly over the cast-off edge of the front piece, overlapping the button bands centrally. Pin in place and then backstitch the pieces together around all of the 4 edges.
3 Turn the cover right sides out and sew buttons on the button band underneath to correspond with the buttonholes.
4 Make a twisted cord (see page 148) using 7 strands, each 6.2m (20ft) long, in Yarn A.
5 Sew the twisted cord around all 4 sides of the cushion, first taking the yarn over the top of the cord and then catching a small stitch into the seam. The ends of the cord can be tucked into the seam so that they are inside the cover. Insert the cushion pad and button the cover closed.

Intarsia knitting – crossing colours

Intarsia knitting involves working colours independently, and, unlike in Fair Isle knitting, the colours are not taken across the back of the work when not being used. Instead, the yarns cross when they meet the neighbouring colours, twisting around each other to prevent a hole being created. This means that when large areas of colour are required, the intarsia crossing method can be used to create a design without thickness and tension problems.

Each area of colour in the design has a ball of yarn, which travels only across that particular area. Even two independent areas of the same colour will have their own supply of yarn. Depending on the size of the area within a design to be knitted in a particular colour, either a whole ball, a bobbin or just an unwound length of yarn can be used. As the fabric is a single thickness, intarsia is very economical on yarn and the colours are very clear.

Care must be taken to keep the stitches tight at the edge of each area. The yarn can be eased as you go along to make the outer stitches of the areas of colour the right shape and size. Intarsia is usually worked in stocking stitch but it can also be worked with textured stitches and cables or combined with Fair Isle to create small areas of a contrast colour with the background colour stranded behind. The argyle or diamond pattern, with an embroidered overcheck, is the most recognizable intarsia design.

1 On a knit row knit up to the colour change. Drop the first colour and then pick up the second. On right-side rows sloping diagonally to the left, and wrong-side rows sloping diagonally to the right, the stepping across of the colour change means that the yarns cross over automatically, as the first yarn is knitted beyond the yarn that you then pick up.

2 On all other diagonals, vertical joins and very large steps, the yarns must be consciously twisted on every row in order to prevent holes in the fabric.

3 On purl rows the technique is the same as for knit but with the yarns being crossed on the side of the fabric now facing you. The blue yarn has been brought under the cream one before working this vertical join.

Pattern instructions

Instructions for intarsia are usually given in the form of a chart. The pattern is shown on a squared grid where one square represents one stitch. It is read in the same way as you knit. The bottom row of the chart, which represents the first row of knitting, is read from right to left, the second row is read from left to right and so on as you move up the chart.

For a stocking-stitch fabric, the first row would be knit stitches and the second row would be purl stitches. Colours on the chart are either represented by symbols or the squares are shaded in the appropriate colour. On a repeating pattern, where the same motif repeats across the piece, only one full repeat may be shown. It will be marked with a heavy outline and an indication that it is to be repeated. There may be extra stitches on either side that are incomplete motifs, added to balance the design within the knitted piece. The chart opposite shows a single, placed motif.

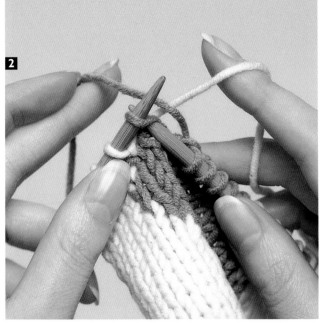

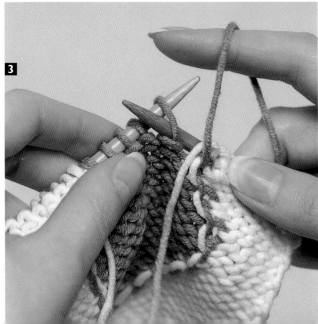

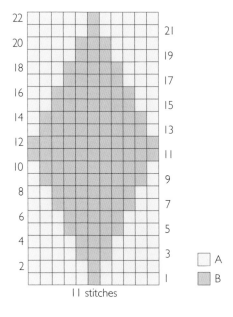

22

21

20

19

18

17

16

15

14

13

12

11

10

9

8

7

6

5

4

3

2

1

11 stitches

☐ A

▨ B

Using the chart, count and knit the stitches in the different areas of the design. Continue counting and changing colours along the row. Once the pattern is established, just glance at the chart to see how the pattern has changed. Put a marker above the row you are working to keep your place and see how it relates to previous ones.

Take care when securing yarn ends at the beginning and end of an area, particularly if it is in the middle of the piece. Leave a long end and pull it up so that the stitch is the same size as the rest. Ensure that the yarn has crossed with the adjacent yarn; if not, sew it through the bar at the base of the adjacent stitch then back across the area it came from. This ensures that the first stitch is complete but the darning is behind fabric of a matching colour.

Kelim-inspired throw Kelims and old woven textiles are a wonderful source of inspiration for intarsia knitting. Kelims in particular have large, geometric motifs that translate well and the colour combinations can be very beautiful. There are no floats to be accidentally pulled and the pattern is presentable on both sides, making it perfect for knitting a patterned throw.

You will need
Pair of 5mm (no 6/US 8) knitting needles

9 x 50g (1¾oz) balls of lambswool/mohair/nylon yarn in lavender (A)

2 x 50g (1¾oz) balls of lambswool/mohair/nylon yarn in white (B)

1 x 50g (1¾oz) balls of lambswool/mohair/nylon yarn in grey (C)

1 x 50g (1¾oz) balls of lambswool/mohair/nylon yarn in pale blue (D)

Sewing needle

Tension
19 stitches and 25 rows over 10cm (4in) square of st st

Finished size
115cm (45½in) square

Working the throw
With 5mm (no 6/US 8) needles and Yarn A, cast on 225 stitches.

1st row of squares 1st row: P45, K45 using Yarns A–D following chart (on page 156), P45, K45 following chart, P45.
2nd row: K45, P45 following chart, K45, P45 following chart, K45.
Rep 1st and 2nd rows to end of chart (58 rows in total).

2nd row of squares 1st row: K45 following chart, P45, K45 following chart, P45, K45 following chart.
2nd row: P45 following chart, K45, P45 following chart, K45, P45 following chart.
Rep 1st row of squares.
Rep 2nd row of squares.
Rep 1st row of squares.
Cast off in stitch, using Yarn A.

Making up the throw
1 Press and block the piece to size. Work a fringe along the cast-on and cast-off edges. For this you will need to cut 226 lengths in Yarn A and 226 lengths in Yarn C, each 14cm (5½in) long.
2 To complete the throw, start from an outer stitch and hook a strand of each colour together through every other stitch (see page 146 for instructions on making a fringe).

Textured Knits

A wide variety of wonderfully pronounced

textures can be created with knitted stitches. We have already seen how crossing stitches form the familiar rope-like appearance of the cable, but there are many more unusual and exciting textural techniques to explore. By knitting into a stitch more than once and then decreasing again at a later stage, areas of fullness can be created in the fabric. Worked in small areas, these extra stitches result in bobbles that stand proud of the knitted surface, or worked across the whole width the fullness forms a ruched effect.

An easy way to create areas of openness in the fabric is to double wrap some of the stitches so that they are enlarged, as if knitted on a much thicker needle. These enlarged stitches will also distort the rows, making them wavy instead of straight. Knitted fabrics can also be gathered with embroidery to create smocking. This technique can be used on stocking stitch, but is even better worked on ribbed fabric, distorting it to form a luxurious, honeycomb surface with real depth. Beads of different materials, shapes and colours can be incorporated during knitting to provide endless creative possibilities. The easiest way to attach beads is on the float created when a stitch is slipped. These slipped-stitch floats are also the basis for butterfly stitch, as demonstrated in the Beaded table runner on page 137.

Bobble knit

The small, round, three-dimensional clusters of stitches that sit on the surface of the knitted fabric are called bobbles. They are very effective, giving a dramatic three-dimensional texture to a knitted surface and are in addition quite deceptively easy to work. To create a bobble, a single stitch is worked into a number of times to form a group of new stitches, which are knitted without knitting background rows, and then the extra stitches are decreased right back to a single stitch. It is these extra knitted stitches that form the pronounced bobble, which stands proud of the main fabric.

Individual methods of doing this vary, with the stitches increased in different ways and the stitches at the edges of the bobble being slipped or decreased at the top in different ways, but the principle remains the same. The greater the number of stitches in a cluster, the more rows knitted and the thicker the yarn, then the bigger the resulting bobble. Smaller bobbles have less definition so they are most frequently worked as an all-over pattern, the most popular being bramble stitch.

Individual bobbles can be worked in stocking stitch or reverse stocking stitch, on a background of stocking stitch, reverse stocking stitch or garter stitch. They work well on their own or in combination with cables, Aran or eyelets. Never make a bobble on the first stitch in a row, as the edges of the fabric will be uneven and difficult to seam. Work the first background stitch after the bobble firmly to give the bobble definition and prevent a hole forming.

Bobbles are always started on right-side rows. To create a stocking-stitch bobble 4 stitches wide and 4 rows deep before decreasing, first work up to the bobble position.

1 Work knit and purl stitches alternately into the next stitch to make 4 new stitches. Insert the needle, wrap the yarn and bring it through the stitch as if to make an ordinary knit stitch but instead of dropping the old stitch from the left needle, take the yarn between the needles to the front of the work. Insert the needle, wrap the yarn and bring it through the stitch as if to make an ordinary purl stitch but still without dropping the old stitch off the left needle. Work two more stitches in the same way, one from the front and one from the back and only then let the original stitch slip off the left needle, leaving the 4 new stitches on the right needle.

2 Turn the work so that the wrong side is facing you and purl the 4 bobble stitches. Turn the work and knit them, then turn the work and purl them, so that there are 3 rows of stocking stitch worked over the bobble stitches.

3 Turn the work so that the right side is facing you. Slip the first bobble stitch from the left to the right needle and then knit the next 3 stitches together.

4 Pass the slipped stitch over the other stitch so that only 1 stitch remains. Continue knitting the rest of the row.

Pattern instructions
A bobble would be written on a pattern as 'Mb' (make bobble) and the exact details of the recommended technique will be given within the instructions.

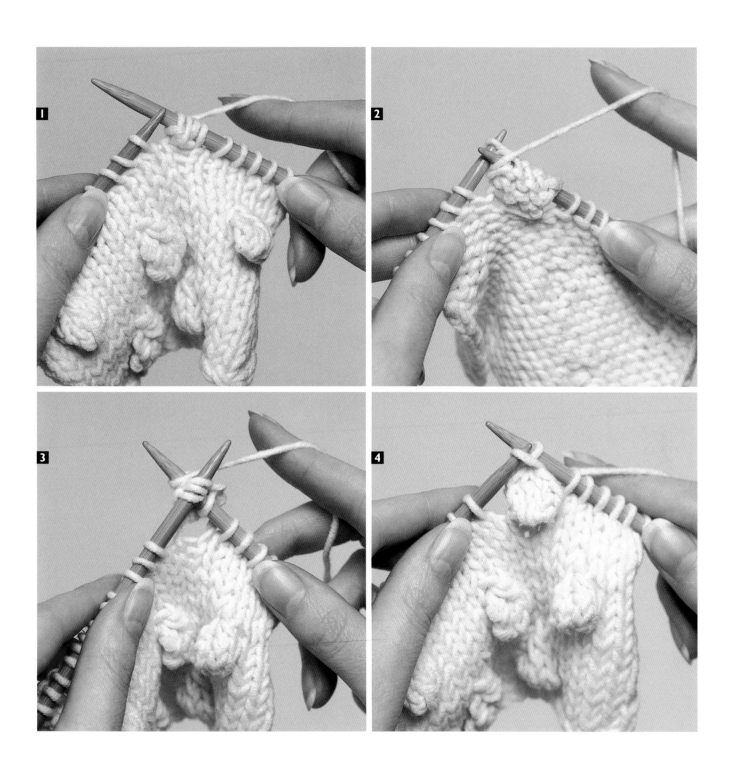

Contrast-bobble cushion Bobbles are usually worked in the background yarn, often in combination with cables. Using a contrast colour or yarn can add definition, bulk or texture to your bobbles and result in a look that is far from traditional. Changing the yarn used for the bobble has no real effect on the overall tension, so experiment with chenille, bouclé or metallic yarn, using a different yarn for every bobble if you wish.

You will need

Pair of 4mm (no 8/US 6) knitting needles

Pair of 3mm (no 11/US 3) knitting needles

5 x 50g (1¾oz) balls of dk merino wool in charcoal (A)

1 x 25g (⅞oz) ball of fine brushed mohair yarn in cream (B) (use two strands)

1 x 25g (⅞oz) ball of fine brushed mohair yarn in caramel (C) (use two strands)

Sewing needle and pins

6 small cream buttons or beads

Card or pom-pom kit

45cm (18in) square cushion pad

Tension

22 stitches and 30 rows over 10cm (4in) square of st st

Finished size

45cm (18in) square

Working the bobbles

Mb = K1, P1, K1, P1 into 1 stitch, work 3 rows of stocking stitch over these 4 stitches, starting with a P row, S1, K3tog, pass slipped stitch over the other stitch. Work the bobbles with a loose loop of yarn running between them on the wrong side. Cut and tie them off when complete.

Working the cushion cover front

With 4mm (no 8/US 6) needles and Yarn A, cast on 93 stitches.
Using Yarn A work 4 rows of st st, starting with a K row.
Bobble repeat **1st bobble row: Using Yarn A – K4, (using Yarn B – Mb, using Yarn A – K13) 6 times, using Yarn B – Mb, using Yarn A – K4.
Using Yarn A, work 7 rows of st st, starting with a P row.
2nd bobble row: Using Yarn A, K11, (using Yarn C – Mb, using Yarn A – K13) 5 times, using Yarn C – Mb, using Yarn A – K11.
Using Yarn A, work 7 rows of st st, starting with a P row **.
Work the bobble repeat, from ** to **, 7 more times.
Rep 1st bobble row once more.
Using Yarn A, work 4 rows of st st, starting with a P row.
Cast off purlwise.

Working the cushion cover back

The cover back is worked in two pieces.
First piece With 4mm (no 8/US 6) needles and Yarn A, cast on 93 stitches.
Using Yarn A, work 4 rows of st st, starting with a K row.
Bobble repeat ***1st bobble row: Using Yarn A – K11, (using Yarn B – Mb, using Yarn A – K13) 5 times, using Yarn B – Mb, using Yarn A – K11.
Using Yarn A, work 7 rows of st st, starting with a P row.
2nd bobble row: Using Yarn A – K4, (using Yarn C – Mb, using Yarn A – K13) 6 times, using Yarn C – Mb, using Yarn A – K4.
Using Yarn A, work 7 rows of st st, starting with a P row ***.
Work the bobble repeat, from *** to *** 2 more times.
Work the bobble repeat once more, up to and including the 2nd bobble row.
Using Yarn A, work 5 rows of st st, starting with a P row.
Change to 3mm (no 11/US 3) needles.
Button band 1st row: K1, (P1, K1) to end.
2nd row: P1, (K1, P1) to end.
Rep 1st and 2nd rows again. (See page 145 for instructions for eyelet buttonholes.)

Buttonhole row: K1, (P1, K1) 5 times, *yon, K2tog, (P1, K1) 6 times *, rep from * to * 4 more times, yon, K2tog, (P1, K1) to the end. Rep 2nd button-band row, followed by 1st and 2nd button-band rows twice more (all without buttonholes).
Cast off in rib.

Second piece With 3mm (no 11/US 3) needles and Yarn A, cast on 93 stitches.

Button band 1st row: K1, (P1, K1) to end. 2nd row: P1, (K1, P1) to end.
Rep 1st and 2nd rows 4 more times.
Change to 4mm (no 8/US 6) needles.
Using Yarn A, work 4 rows of st st, starting with a K row.

Bobble repeat ****1st bobble row: Using Yarn A – K4, (using Yarn C – Mb, using Yarn A – K13) 6 times, using Yarn C – Mb, using Yarn A – K4.
Using Yarn A, work 7 rows of st st, starting with a P row.
2nd bobble row: Using Yarn A – K11, (using Yarn B – Mb, using Yarn A – K13) 5 times, using Yarn B – Mb, using Yarn A – K11.
Using Yarn A, work 7 rows of st st, starting with a P row ****.
Work the bobble repeat, from **** to **** 2 more times.
Work the bobble repeat once more, up to and including the 2nd bobble row.
Using Yarn A, work 4 rows of st st, starting with a P row.
Cast off purlwise.

Making up the cushion cover

1 Press and block the front and back pieces to size. Then lay out the front piece, right side up and the first back piece (with buttonholes) on top, right side down, with the cast-on edge over the cast-on edge of the front piece.

2 Next, place the second back piece on top, right side down, with the cast-off edge over the cast-off edge of the front piece, overlapping the button bands in the centre. Pin then backstitch the pieces together around all 4 edges, taking care to match the lines of bobbles.

3 Turn the cover right sides out and sew buttons on the button band underneath to correspond with the buttonholes.

4 Make 4 small pom-poms, 2 in cream mohair (Yarn B) and 2 in caramel mohair (Yarn C), using a ring with an outer diameter of 4.5cm (1¾in) and an inner circle diameter of 2cm (⅞in) (see page 148 for instructions). Leave tails of about 10cm (4in) when binding the centre of the pom-pom and use them to attach one to each corner. Finally, insert the cushion pad and button the cover closed.

Double-wrap stitch

A very long stitch can be made by wrapping the yarn more than once around the needle, then knitting only into the first wrap on the next line. This is an easy technique for making a fabric with a degree of openness. Whole rows can be double-wrapped to create open stripes, although working these rows with a much thicker needle (called oddpin knitting) can produce the same effect more easily. When selected groups of stitches within a row are double-wrapped, those on either side will distort to form waves. Areas of elongated stitches will be loose and stretchy so are best broken up with tighter, normal stitches

In this sample we are working reverse stocking stitch with 4 normal stitches and then 4 double-wrapped stitches, repeating across the row. The next row (a right-side row) is purled. The elongated stitches are more visible from the reverse stocking-stitch side of the fabric. Knitting only alternate rows with elongated stitches makes the fabric easier to control and the effect more pronounced.

1 Work up to the stitch that is to be double wrapped. This can be either a knit or purl stitch. Work it in the usual way but wrap the yarn twice around the needle and draw both wraps through the old loop so that they sit side by side on the right needle.

2 On the following row work into the first wrap only.

3 Drop both wraps from the left needle, producing 1 elongated stitch.

Pattern instructions
A double-wrap stitch would be written on a pattern as:
Ky2rn3, meaning knit next 3 stitches winding yarn twice around needle.
Py2rn3, meaning purl next 3 stitches winding yarn twice around needle.
or for an even larger stitch as:
Ky3rn1, meaning knit next stitch winding yarn 3 times around needle.

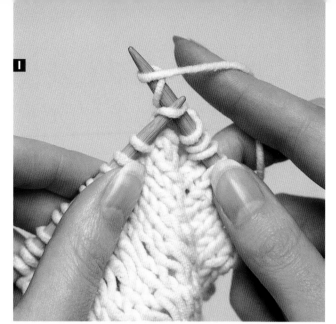

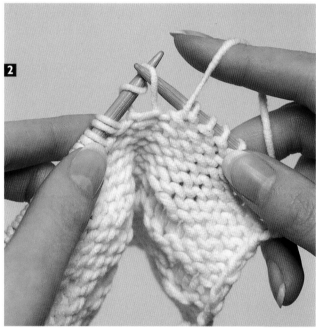

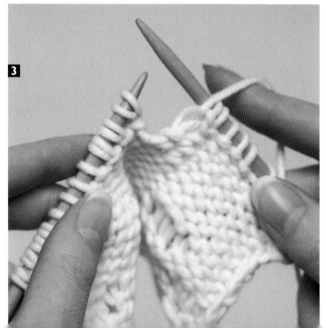

Double-wrap-stitch throw

The combination of elongated stitches and a hairy yarn make this throw beautifully open, light and airy. The contrast-coloured edging has some simple increases and decreases at the ends, which form neat, mitred corners (see page 143 for instructions on making a mitred-corner knitted edging). Double-wrap stitches are worked within raised welts of reverse stocking stitch for added texture.

You will need

Pair of 5mm (no 6/US 8) knitting needles

10 x 50g (1¾oz) balls of mohair/lambswool mix yarn in dark brown (A)

2 x 50g (1¾oz) balls of mohair/lambswool mix yarn in dark red (B)

Sewing needle and pins

Tension

18 stitches and 20 rows over 10cm (4in) square of patterned fabric

Finished size

105 x 130cm (41½ x 51in)

Working the throw

With 5mm (no 6/US 8) needles and Yarn A, cast on 184 stitches.
Work 8 rows of st st, starting with a K row.
*9th row: P5, (Py2rn3, P3) to last 5 stitches, Py2rn3, P2.
10th row: K to end.
11th row: P2, (Py2rn3, P3) to last 2 stitches, P2.
12th row: K to end.
13th row: P5, (Py2rn3, P3) to last 5 stitches, Py2rn3, P2.
14th row: K to end.
Work 6 rows of st st, starting with a K row *.
From * to * forms the patt. Rep patt 21 times.
Work 2 rows of st st, starting with a K row.
Cast off.

Working the edging

With 5mm (no 6/US 8) needles and Yarn B, cast on 180 sts.
**1st row: K, inc into 2nd and 2nd to last sts.
2nd row: P to end.

3rd row: K, inc into 2nd and 2nd to last sts.
4th row: K to end.
5th row: K, dec into 2nd and 2nd to last sts.
6th row: P to end.
7th row: K, dec into 2nd and 2nd to last sts.
Cast off purlwise **.
Work 2 pieces.
With 5mm (no 6/US 8) needles and Yarn B, cast on 217 sts
Work 2 more pieces from ** to **.

Making up the throw

1 Press and block the throw and edging pieces. Take alternate long and short edging strips and oversew the pointed ends together to form mitred joins within a continuous loop.
2 Fold the edging in half lengthways along the line of purl stitches and line up the mitres with the throw corners. Next, sandwich the throw between the 2 layers of edging. Pin then sew in position with a small running stitch through all 3 layers using Yarn B.

Smocked knitting

Knitted fabrics can be smocked in the same way as woven fabrics. It is an effect that can be created during knitting with the aid of a cable needle or with a sewing needle, after knitting is complete. The latter technique is a little slower but the tension is easier to control and it gives the option of using a contrast yarn for the ties. Smocking works particularly well on ribbed fabrics because of their natural tendency to curl. Two oversewn stitches draw together the knit stitches on either side of a number of purl stitches. When the tie above is staggered so that it falls between the ties below, the fabric distorts into a lovely honeycomb appearance.

The knitted columns are usually one or two stitches wide, and are separated by an odd number of purl stitches. Widely spaced columns tend to be worked with a greater number of rows between ties, therefore making increasingly deep honeycombs. Stitch two rows of oversewing at a time so that the thread zigzags along the back of the fabric and the knitting retains some give widthways. The location of the ties can be marked as you knit, with knit stitches within the appropriate purl areas. The marker stitches will be covered when the knit stitches on either side are drawn together over the top.

Knit the basic fabric in the usual way, in this case a 3 purl and 1 knit rib with additional knit stitches to mark the point at which the ribs will be stitched together. Beads could be added so that they sit with one on top of each of the smocking stitches. Reverse stocking-stitch welts can be smocked in a similar way to ribs. The raised rows are drawn together and stitched at intervals zig-zagging vertically up the work.

1 Bring the needle up to the front of the work, at the marker point, to the left of the knit rib. Stitch into the right of the second rib and back up to the left of the first one.
2 Pull the ribs together by tightening the stitch.
3 Take the needle down to the back of the work, to the right of the second rib and bring it back to the front some rows higher, at the marker point and to the left of the second rib. Stitch the second and third ribs together in the same way as before, then take the needle down to the right of the third rib and up again some rows below, at the marker point, to the left of the third rib.

Pattern instructions
A smocked design stitched after knitting is complete would be written on a pattern as a sequence of knit and purl stitches to form the basic fabric. There would then be detailed instructions on how to complete the embroidery.

Smocked knitted fabric becomes heavy, firm and about 25 per cent narrower after it has been stitched, so knit an extra-large tension swatch to take this into account.

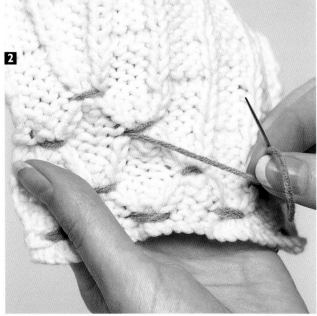

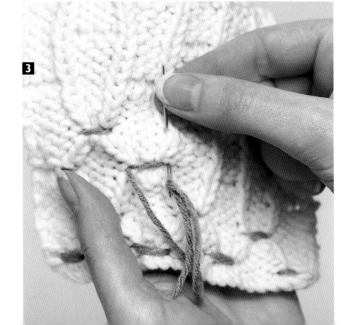

Honeycomb floor cushion

Honeycomb floor cushion The deeply textured stitch that makes up the front piece of this floor cushion is worked in a soft, full, cotton-mix yarn. The intricacy of this fabric contrasts with the side and back panels of the cover, which are worked very simply in stocking stitch.

You will need

Pair of 5mm (no 6/US 8) knitting needles

8 x 50g (1¾oz) balls cotton/acrylic yarn in brown (A)

1 x 50g (1¾oz) balls cotton/acrylic yarn in purple (B)

Sewing needle and pins

45 x 55 x 10cm (18 x 22 x 4in) 33/190 grade foam cushion inner

Tension

17 stitches and 22 rows over 10cm (4in) square of st st

20 stitches and 24 rows over 10cm (4in) square of patterned fabric (once stitching completed)

Finished size

45 x 55 x 10cm (18 x 22 x 4in)

Working the cushion cover front

With 5mm (no 6/US 8) needles and Yarn A, cast on a total of 93 stitches.

1st row: P4, (K5, P3) 10 times, K5, P4.
2nd row: K4, (P1, K3) 21 times, P1, K4.
3rd row: P4, (K1, P3) 21 times, K1, P4.
4th row: Rep 2nd row.
5th row: P1, K4, (P3, K5) 10 times, P3, K4, P1.
6th row: Rep 2nd row.
7th row: Rep 3rd row.
8th row: Rep 2nd row.
Rep 1st to 8th rows 15 more times.
Rep 1st row once more.
Cast off.

Using Yarn B, oversew the ribs together over the knit stitch markers, 2 rows at a time, so that the thread zigzags across the back of the fabric. The final row will have to be sewn singly, leaving loose floats between.

Working the cushion cover back

With 5mm (no 6/US 8) needles and Yarn A, cast on a total of 78 stitches.
Work 122 rows of st st.
Cast off.

Working the sides

With 5mm (no 6/US 8) needles and Yarn A, cast on a total of 96 stitches.
Work 22 rows of st st.
Cast off.
Work 2 pieces.

Working the ends

With 5mm (no 6/US 8) needles and Yarn A, cast on a total of 78 stitches.
Work 22 rows of st st.
Cast off.
Work 2 pieces.

Making up the cushion cover

1 Press and block all 6 pieces to size. With right sides facing, backstitch the end and the side pieces together alternately, end to end, to make a loop.

2 Matching the seams to the appropriate corners and with right sides together, backstitch the strip around all 4 edges of the front piece.

3 Attach the back piece in just the same way to the other edge of the strip but on this occasion leave one of the shorter edges unstitched.

4 Turn the cover right sides out, insert the foam pad, then stitch the final edge closed.

Ruching

Increases and decreases are most commonly used to shape knitted pieces. Increasing the number of stitches widens the fabric, whereas decreasing the number of stitches narrows it. They can also be used to create stitch patterns such as ruching. There are other ways of increasing, but by this method each stitch in a row is made into two by knitting and then purling into the same stitch. Some rows later, stitches are knitted together in twos to bring the stitches back to the original number. The overall width of the piece stays the same but in the areas where there are more stitches the fabric is wider, causing it to form rippled or gathered bands.

Working increases on a knit row
1 Knit the stitch in the usual way but do not drop the old loop from the left needle.
2 Take the yarn between the needles to the front of the work and purl the stitch. Slip the old stitch off the left needle, leaving 2 new loops on the right needle. Take the yarn between the needles again to the back of the work to knit the next stitch.

Working increases on a purl row
Work in the same way as for the knit row but purling and then knitting the stitch before slipping the old stitch off the left needle.

Working decreases on a knit row
1 Insert the needle from left to right through 2 stitches instead of 1.
2 Pass the yarn around the needles in the usual way and knit the 2 stitches together as 1 to create 1 new loop on the right needle.

Working decreases on a purl row
Work as for the knit stitch but this time inserting the right needle from right to left through the 2 stitches.

Pattern instructions
An increase is written on a pattern as 'inc 1 stitch' or 'inc in next stitch'. A decrease could be written as 'K2tog' (knit 2 together) or 'p2tog' (purl 2 together), or sometimes just 'dec 1 stitch'.

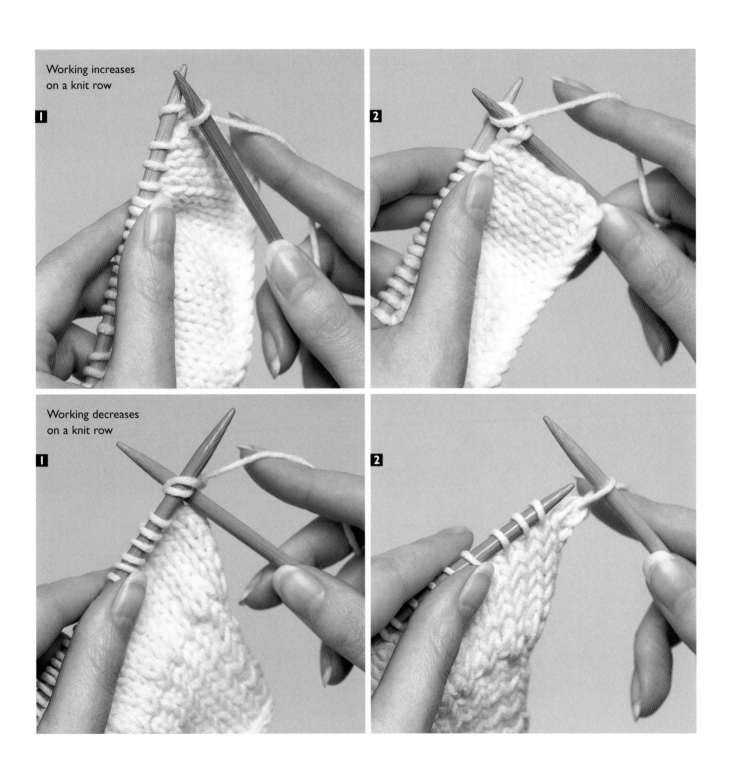

Working increases
on a knit row

1

2

Working decreases
on a knit row

1

2

Ruched throw The rustic, handcrafted qualities of this design are created with a soft, slightly irregular yarn and simple, untrimmed edges. The surface decoration between the bands of folded fabric is worked in cross stitch, a traditional embroidery stitch used in an unusual way. In this example, the regular flecks of peppermint-blue cross stitch increase the overall textural interest.

You will need

3 4mm (no 8/US 6) knitting needles or 4mm (no 8/US 6) circular needles

12 x 50g (1¾oz) balls of dk woollen yarn in white (A)

Stitch stopper or cork

1 x 50g (1¾oz) balls of dk woollen yarn in pale blue (B) (for embroidery)

Sewing needle and pins

Tension

18 stitches and 30 rows over 10cm (4in) square of patterned fabric

Finished size

100 x 138cm (39½ x 54½in)

Working the throw

With 4mm (no 8/US 6) needles and Yarn A, cast on 180 stitches.
Work 10 rows of st st, starting with a K row.

Ruching

*1st row: Inc into every stitch.
Work 9 rows of st st, starting with a P row.
Next row: K2tog to end.
Work 9 rows of st st, starting with a P row *.
Work these 20 rows, from * to *, 19 more times.
Cast off.

After you have increased into every stitch, there will be a total of 360 stitches, too many to fit comfortably on a standard-length needle, so you may wish to use a third needle. When the first right needle is full, stop the end with a stitch stopper and start knitting the remaining stitches from the left needle to a third needle in the right hand. Continue using three needles until the number of stitches is decreased allowing you to return to 2 needles. Alternatively, knit the whole throw on circular needles.

Making up the throw

1 Press and block the throw, taking care not to flatten the ruched areas, especially the edges.
2 Using Yarn B, work cross stitch down the centre of the unruched stripes. Work the stitch across 2 rows and on alternate groups of 2 stitches, starting 1 stitch in from the edge. Anchor the stitching yarn on the back of the throw with a couple of small stitches. Bring the needle up to the front at the top right of the group of 4 stitches and take it back down to the back at the bottom left. Bring it back up to the front at the bottom right and down to the back at the top left. Carry the yarn along the reverse of the fabric for the next group of 4 stitches and repeat until you are 1 stitch away from the other edge. Anchor the thread with small stitches.

Bead knitting

Beads, sequins and other decorative objects can be incorporated in a fabric as it is being knitted. Slipping a stitch with the yarn on the right side of the knitting creates a bar on which a bead can be hung without distorting the surrounding stitches. Slip more than one stitch for a bigger bead. The effect can be a beautiful, random, all-over shimmer or a regular pattern of larger beads. Be aware that beaded knits can be heavy, although this can be used to advantage, to weight the edges of throws, tablecloths and openings.

Fabrics should be knitted to quite a firm tension to avoid the beads slipping through to the wrong side. To keep edges neat and to avoid beads getting in the way of seams, beads should not be worked right up to the edges of a piece. Bead-knitted fabrics have areas where knitted loops are visible on the right side of the work. If only beads are visible on the right side of the fabric, this is termed close-bead knitting, which was very popular in the eighteenth century for collars and cuffs, but is made by a different technique.

Use a yarn that is strong enough to hold the weight of the bead and a bead with a big-enough hole to take the yarn. Thread all of the beads that you will need on to the yarn before starting to knit, otherwise the yarn will have to be broken or the ball unwound to add beads from the other end. If a design involves beads of different sizes or colours, thread them on to the yarn in the reverse order to the order in which they will be used; that is, the first bead to be threaded will be the last bead to be knitted.

Working beads with slipped stitches
A bead can be placed on the surface of stocking stitch from either a right-side or a wrong-side row. Working on a wrong-side row is easier as the direction that the needle is inserted into the loop is the same whether for purling or slipping.

1 Thread the beads onto the yarn before you begin knitting, using cotton thread and a needle.
2 On a wrong-side row work up to the bead position, then take the yarn between the needles to the other side of the work (what will be the right side of the piece). Bring the bead up close to the last worked stitch on the right needle.
3 Slip the next stitch from the left needle to the right.
4 Bring the yarn between the needles to the side of the work facing you and purl up to the next slipped stitch. The bead should be left sitting in front of the slipped stitch, on the stocking-stitch side of the fabric.

To place a bead on the surface of stocking stitch on a right-side row, bring the yarn forward between the needles, bring up the bead, slip a stitch, and return the yarn between the needles to the other side.

The hole in the bead will probably be too small for a needle with a big-enough eye to carry the yarn to pass through. So, using a needle fine enough to pass through the bead, thread it with both ends of a short length of sewing thread. Pass the yarn through the loop that this creates, folding it back on itself. Now thread the beads on to the needle and push them down the thread and on to the yarn.

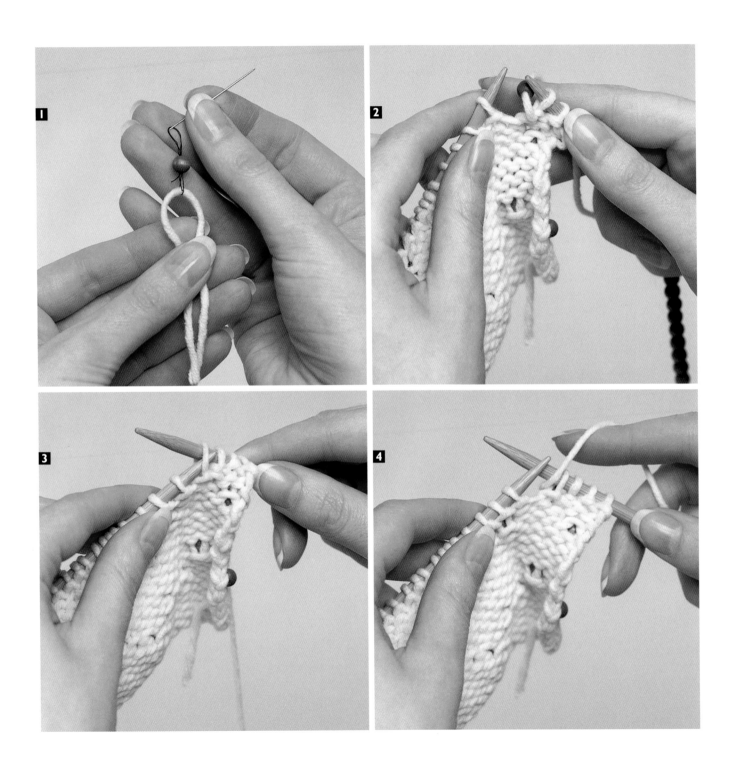

Butterfly slipped stitch

Slipped-stitch floats, meaning the strands of yarn that have been carried across the back or front of slipped stitches (see page 90 for instructions), are the basis of this decorative stitch. The first stage of the butterfly slipped stitch is to slip an odd number of stitches to leave three floats on the right side of the fabric. A stitch is then looped centrally under the floats as knitting progresses, pulling the floats upwards in the process to form a distinctive butterfly shape. The butterfly slipped stitch can be worked as a decorative stitch in its own right or can be combined with beads placed on any or all of the floating strands.

1 Purl up to the stitches that are to be slipped. Take the yarn between the needles to the other side of the work (what will be the right side of the piece). Slip an odd number of stitches (in this case 5) with the strand across the right side of the fabric, then bring the yarn back to the side facing you and purl the next 5 stitches, repeating across the fabric. Knit the next row as normal. Repeat these 2 rows, 2 more times (leaving 2 beads on the middle of the three strands for a beaded butterfly like the one shown).

2 On the central stitch of the knit row above the strands, take the right needle under and up behind the strands (between the 2 beads) and then insert it into the next stitch.

3 Wrap the yarn around the needle as you would a normal knit stitch. Pull the new loop through the previous stitch then down, under and out from beneath the strands.

4 Pull the new loop up into place on the left needle and continue knitting.

Pattern instructions

Instructions may be given in words or a chart, depending on the complexity and repetitiveness of the design. Written instructions might say 'wyab' (with yarn at back) or 'wyaf' (with yarn at front), meaning bring the yarn between the needles to the other side of the work so that the float is created on the correct side of the fabric. The position of a bead would be written on a pattern as 'PB' (place bead). On a chart a slip stitch is often shown as a horizontal line, and the position of a bead would be given with a symbol such as a large dot placed within a square, representing a knitted stitch with a bead sitting in front.

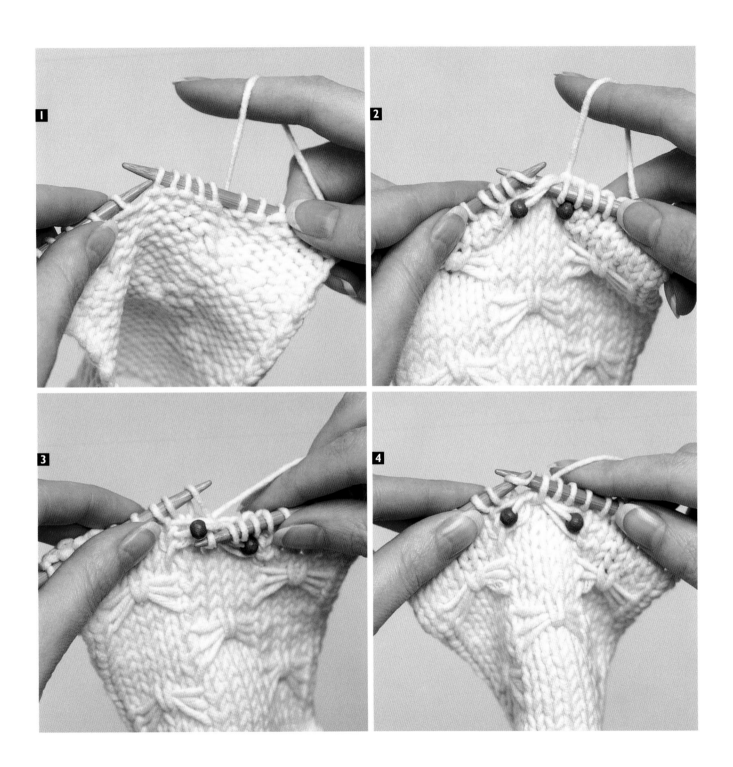

Beaded table runner Glossy silk yarn embellished with glass beads makes a magical runner for the dining table on a special occasion, a side table or the mantelpiece. Beaded fringes at both ends finish it off beautifully. The same design would look very different worked in a linen or cotton yarn with wooden beads for a more everyday, natural look.

You will need

Pair of 3mm (no 11/US 3) knitting needles

4 x 50g (1¾oz) balls of silk yarn in silver

Sewing needle and pins

570 spherical 3mm (⅛in) diameter beads in various colours

32 drop beads in various colours

Tension

28 stitches and 38 rows over 10cm (4in) square of st st

Finished size

28 x 141cm (11 x 55½in)

Working the runner

Begin by threading 173 spherical beads each on to two balls of yarn, in a random mix of colours. The beaded balls will be the first and last of the 4 balls to be knitted.

With 3mm (no 11/US 3) needles and one of the beaded balls of yarn, cast on a total of 79 stitches.
Border – *1st row: K to end.
2nd row: P3, (wyab, sl1, PB, P3) to end.
3rd row: K to the end.
4th row: P1, (wyab, sl1, PB, P3) 19 times, wyab, sl1, PB, P1.
Rep 1st to 4th rows once more.
Rep 1st and 2nd rows once more *.
Work the butterflies as indicated on Chart 1, rows 1–37, repeating as directed (see page 157).
Work the butterflies up the sides of the runner as indicated on Chart 2, rows 38–55. Each repeat measures 3.2cm (1¼in). Add or subtract rows here to adjust the length.
Work the butterfly design with no beads as indicated on Chart 1, rows 20–37.
Work the butterfly design with beads as indicated on Chart 1, rows 2–19.
Next row: P to end.
Repeat border design from * to *.
Cast off.

Making up the runner

1 Press and block the knitted piece to size, paying particular attention to the edges and avoiding the beads. Cut 16 lengths of yarn each approximately 25cm (10in) long, and split each length in half by separating out the individual strands that it constitutes.
2 Take 1 of the split pieces and thread 6 spherical beads, 1 drop bead, then 1 spherical bead on to it.
3 Next, take the yarn back through the drop bead and the 6 spherical beads to complete a single beaded string.
4 To complete the runner, make 32 of these strings and sew 1 into the second and every fifth subsequent stitch along both the cast-on and cast-off edges to make a fringe.

Finishing

Tying up loose ends

Everyone drops stitches or makes a mistake at some time so you need to know how to put them right. Remember that the further back down the rows a mistake is, the harder it is to correct. Finishing off your work by blocking and pressing and darning in ends, as well as adding buttons, buttonholes and fastenings will transform the curled and rather untidy-looking squares of fabric you have knitted into beautiful soft furnishings.

Picking up dropped stitches

Attend to any mistakes immediately, as the further back they are, the harder they will be to correct. Catch a dropped loop with a safety pin as soon as it is spotted to prevent it running further. Dropped stitches can be recovered even if a ladder runs down through a number of rows. To re-form the stitches, work up the strands of the ladder in the right order, re-forming them in line with the knit and purl sequence of the pattern. There is an increased risk of dropping stitches and ladders will run far more quickly with a smooth, regular yarn.

Repairing a knit stitch

I To repair a knit stitch on the side of the fabric facing you, insert the right needle in the stitch from the side facing you, then over and behind the first strand of the ladder.
2 Draw the strand down and through the loop, keeping the needle through the newly formed stitch to prevent it running back. If the next stitch above is another knit stitch, remove the needle and reinsert it from the front.

Repairing a purl stitch

I To repair a purl stitch on the side of the fabric facing you, insert the right needle in the stitch

from the side facing away from you and then over and behind the first strand of the ladder.
2 Draw the strand down and through the loop, keeping the needle through the newly formed stitch to prevent it running back. If the stitch above is another purl stitch, remove the needle and reinsert it from the back. If you find it easier, you could turn the work and repair it as a knit stitch. The loops can also be drawn through with a crochet hook.

Small errors, such as split yarn or mistakes in the pattern on previous rows, can be easily corrected. Work up to the stitch directly above, then drop it, allowing a ladder to run in a controlled way down to the mistake. Put it right and then rework the ladder with a needle in just the same way as for a dropped stitch. To correct larger errors, you may have to remove the work from the needles and pull the rows back to a point before the mistake was made. To pick up the stitches, use a needle that is a couple of sizes smaller than those you are using, as the loops will slide on more easily. It is often easier to slip the stitches quickly onto the needle and untwist any facing in the wrong direction while knitting the next row.

Blocking and pressing

This process sets the yarn in shape within the fabric through the use of steam or water and relaxes the tension between the loops so that the fabric lays flat. Blocking involves pinning the pieces of knitting out to shape, right side up, on a flat, soft surface. Squares and rectangles can be pinned out to shape much more easily by working on top of a chequered cloth using the woven lines as a guide. Spread out the knitting until it reaches the measurements in the instructions. It should be under slight tension but not overstretched. Pay particular attention to the edges, as this will make sewing up easier.

Pin all around the edges, starting with the corners. Dampen the pieces of fabric with a cold-water mist spray or a damp towel laid over the top, then allow them to dry naturally. Alternatively, you can press the pieces with an iron held over a damp cloth. Do not let the full weight of the iron rest on the work, and lift then reapply the iron – do not slide it. You could also use a steam iron held just above the fabric, letting the steam penetrate and relax the fabric. Take great care not to flatten textured yarns and

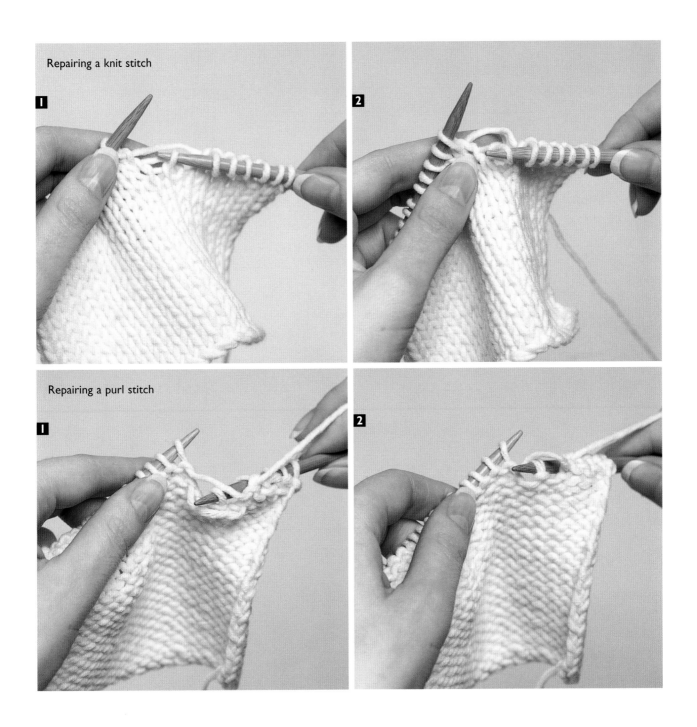

Repairing a knit stitch

1

2

Repairing a purl stitch

1

2

stitches with too much pressing. There may be some information on the ball band about how the yarn is best blocked or pressed. To achieve the best results, you could experiment with a sample piece of knitting.

When a yarn changes character (for example, during the washing of the denim yarn used for the Striped shoulder bag on page 66, or the fluffy angora yarn used for the Cabled heart hot-water bottle cover on page 84), wash the pieces, then pin them out to shape and allow them all to dry naturally before then sewing them together.

Darning in ends

The ends of yarn at the beginning of the cast-on, at the end of the cast-off and where a new ball of yarn is introduced must be neatly darned into the back of the fabric. It is particularly important that this is done with great care on throws where both sides will be visible. Thread the end of the yarn through a large-eyed needle and then pass it through the back of 5 or 6 stitches horizontally, vertically or diagonally, whichever one shows the least.

Seams

Lay the pieces to be seamed either right sides or wrong sides together as appropriate, then pin along the length of the seam. Carefully match the pattern, row to row along the sides and stitch to stitch along the top and bottom. Sew through the centre of the corresponding stitches on the 2 pieces, 1 stitch in from the edge (or half a stitch on very heavyweight knits).

If the yarn is relatively smooth and not too bulky, then use the same yarn to sew the pieces together as the one that they are knitted in. Otherwise, you could use a smooth, colour-matched knitting yarn, but never a sewing thread because this will not stretch with the fabric.

Sewing a backstitched seam

Most knitted soft furnishings can be backstitched together, as the seam this produces gives a strong, firm edge.

I Backstitch is formed by making a long stitch forward, followed by a short stitch back (see below left).

Sewing a running-stitch seam

Running stitch seams are useful for raised seams where wrong sides are together and both sides of the stitching will be visible. This is because the stitch has exactly the same appearance on both sides.

I A small running stitch is formed by passing the needle up and slightly diagonally forward through the layers of fabric, then advancing by at least half a knitting stitch, passing the needle back down and slightly diagonally forward through the layers of fabric (see below centre).

Sewing an overstitched seam

Overstitched seams can be worked with the wrong sides of the fabric together to create an attractive decorative finish.

I An overstitched seam is formed by passing the needle through the layers of fabric, then bringing the yarn over the edges and inserting the needle again, from the same side as previously but advanced by a short distance. It is important that the stitches are regularly spaced (see below right).

Sewing a backstitched seam

Sewing a running-stitch seam

Sewing an overstitched seam

Edgings

When not included in a seam, edges will usually need finishing so that they do not curl and the item retains its shape.

Knitted mitred-corner edging strip

1 Oversew the pointed ends of the mitred strips together with tiny stitches, catching only half of the outer knitted stitches.

2 To attach the strip to the piece, fold the strip in half along the purl line and sandwich the edge to be covered between the 2 layers of the edging strip. Stitch in position with a very small running stitch through all 3 layers in the same yarn as the edging strip.

Ribbon mitred corner

1 Fold the ribbon in half along its length, wrong sides together, and iron in a crease. Then iron in a crease across the width of the ribbon, right sides together, at each corner point. Using sewing thread, backstitch a right-angled seam through both layers of ribbon, coming to a point in the centre.

2 To attach the ribbon to the piece, turn the seam to the inside and, folding the ribbon along the pre-creased line, sandwich the edge to be covered between the 2 layers of ribbon. Stitch in position with a small running stitch and sewing thread that matches the ribbon.

Buttons and buttonholes

Fastenings with buttons are great for knitted items because they anchor the edges securely, but still allow the fabric to stretch and move. Buttons can also be decorative, so choose a design that works with the colour and texture

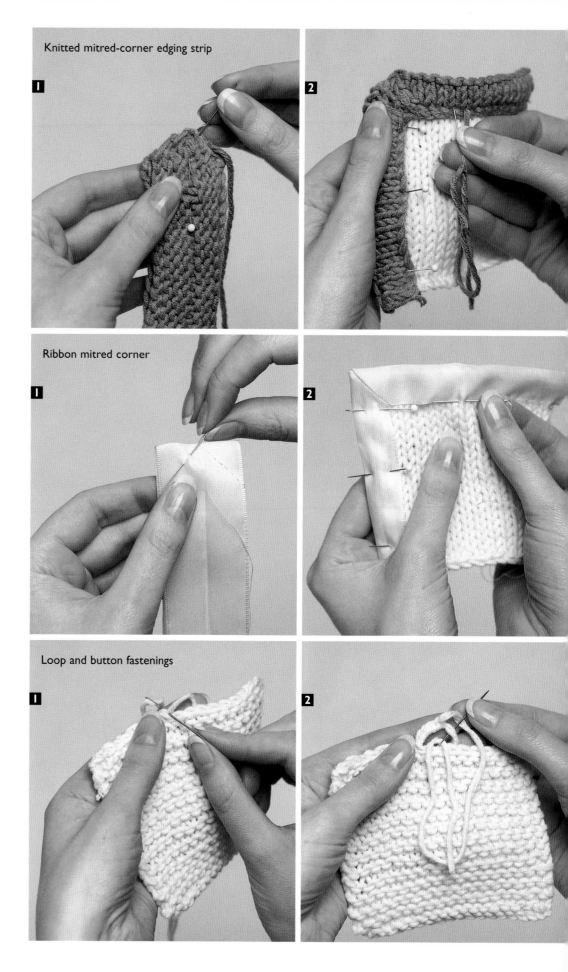

Knitted mitred-corner edging strip

Ribbon mitred corner

Loop and button fastenings

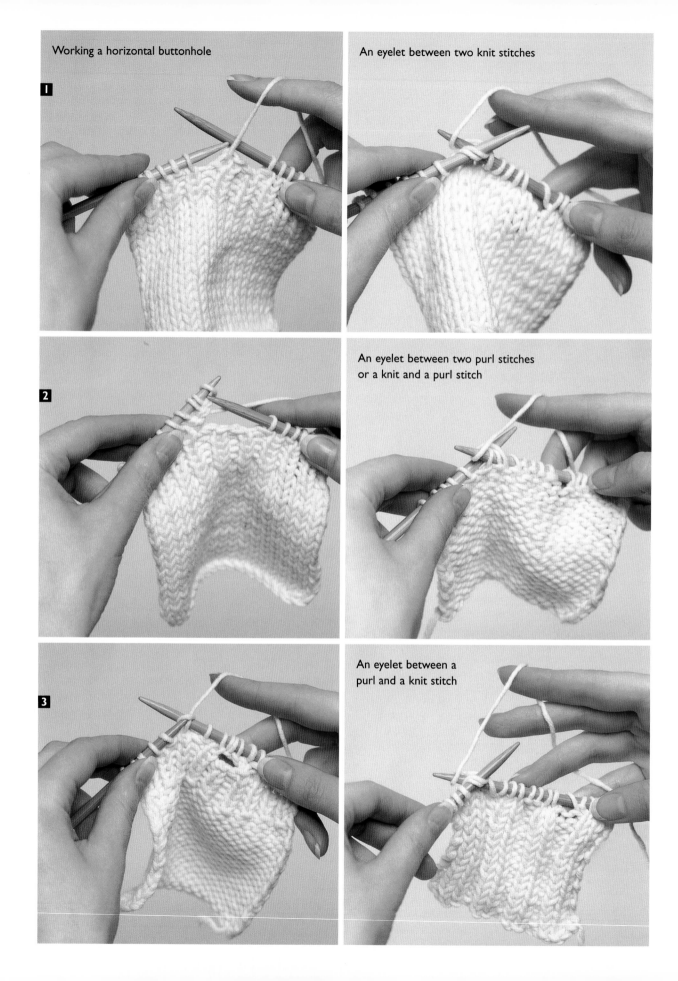

Working a horizontal buttonhole

1

An eyelet between two knit stitches

2

An eyelet between two purl stitches
or a knit and a purl stitch

3

An eyelet between a
purl and a knit stitch

of the piece. Either buy your buttons before making your buttonholes or make them first and find buttons to fit. Most knitted fabrics need a shanked button (with a loop or stem at the back that raises the button so it sits neatly on the fabric), so buy one or make a shank from thread as you sew the button on. Use the knitting yarn, or a finer colour-matched yarn if the former is uneven or too thick.

Secure the yarn with a small backstitch, then sew through the holes in the button with 4 or 5 stitches. Use a spacer such as a cable needle between the button and the fabric as you sew, then remove it and wrap the yarn around the thread to make a shank before fastening off the yarn. The shank accommodates the bulkiness of the fabric, enabling the button to sit smoothly on top of the 2 layers. Press-stud fastenings are another option, with a button sewn on top for decoration.

Loop and button fastenings
(see page 143)

Loop buttonholes are attached to the edge of the fabric and are good for the beginner as they can be added once knitting is complete.

1 Stitch a double loop of thread on the edge of the outer layer of fabric.
2 Reinforce the loop with blanket stitch. Anchor the thread and pass the needle under the double loop and over the stitching yarn. Pull the yarn so that the resulting 'knot' sits firmly on the double loop. Continue in this way, pulling each knot up to the preceding one until the whole of the double loop is covered.

Working a horizontal buttonhole

A number of stitches are cast off on a right-side row, and are then cast back on in the next row to create a slit-shaped hole. On 1 × 1 rib a buttonhole will usually be worked over an odd number of stitches, starting and finishing with a knit stitch on the right side. On 2 × 2 rib a buttonhole will usually be worked over an even number of stitches; for example, a buttonhole 4 stitches wide would usually be worked over 1 purl, 2 knit and 1 purl stitches.

1 On a right-side row work right up to the buttonhole position, cast off the required number of stitches (in this case 3), then work the rest of the row.
2 On the next row, work up to the cast-off stitches, turn the work and cast on the same number using the cable method.
3 Turn the work again and continue knitting the rest of the row.

Eyelets

These holes are used to thread cord through, to make picot edges or buttonholes. The size of the eyelet will depend on the thickness of the yarn and the needle. Eyelet buttonholes are used for small buttons in combination with light- to medium-weight fabrics and on heavy fabrics where a horizontal buttonhole, worked over a number of stitches, would be too large.

Working an eyelet

A hole is created by taking the yarn over the needle, forming a loop that is then knitted in the next row. As a new stitch has been formed, 2 stitches are then knitted together to decrease

the number of stitches by 1, keeping the number of stitches constant. The way an eyelet is worked depends on whether the stitches before and after it are knitted or purled.

An eyelet between two knit stitches

In a pattern this is written as 'yfwd' or 'yf' (yarn forward) or 'yo' (yarn over) and then K2 tog (knit 2 together).

1 Bring the yarn forward between the needles so it is below the right needle and knit the next 2 stitches together, passing the yarn up the front and back over the top of the right needle.

An eyelet between two purl stitches
or a knit and a purl stitch

In a pattern this is written as 'yrn' (yarn round needle) or 'yo' (yarn over) and then P2 tog (purl 2 together).

1 Take the yarn over the top of the right needle, then under it to the front again and purl the next two stitches together. For a knit to a purl, first bring the yarn forward between the needles so that it is under the right needle before wrapping in the same way as shown. This is sometimes called 'yfrn' (yarn forward and round needle).

An eyelet between a purl and a knit stitch

In a pattern this is written as 'yon' (yarn over needle) or 'yo' (yarn over) and then K2 tog (knit 2 together).

1 Take the yarn over the top of the needle, then knit the next two stitches together.

Finishing touches

Adding details such as fringes, pom-poms, tassels and cords can really distinguish a knitted item when the style calls for it. If you are planning to add a decorative edging or some tassels to your piece, bear in mind that it will affect your yarn requirements.

Fringes

Knotted fringes, which are a series of tassels worked directly onto an edge, make a lovely decorative finish for blankets and throws. They have a slightly bohemian, informal character mimicking the frayed edge of a woven fabric. Make a couple of tassels first and tie them in place to make sure you are happy with the effect, before cutting all the lengths of yarn.

Making a fringe

Wrap yarn around a piece of card to produce a number of strands of the same length. The strands must be at least twice the length of the desired fringe plus 2cm (¾in). Put 2 or 3 pieces of yarn together and fold them in half. The number of strands that you will need depends on how thick you would like the fringe to be and how closely together each of the knots are worked.

1 Insert a crochet hook from the back, up through the edge of the work, and then draw the folded end of the strands down through the knitting.
2 Draw the loose ends of the strands through the loop at the folded end and pull it up to form a knot. When all of the loops are completed, tidy them so that they are even and trim the ends straight across.

Tassels

Effective for decorating the corners of cushions and throws, tassels can also be attached to the ends of a twisted cord.

Making a tassel

1 Wrap yarn around a piece of card of the same width that you would like the tassel to be in length.
2 Thread a needle with a length of yarn and pass it between the yarn and the card. Tie it firmly at one end, bringing all the wraps of yarn together and leaving long, uncut tails of the yarn hanging free.
3 Cut across the strands at the opposite end of the card.
4 Use one of the ends of yarn left previously to wind around the strands at a short distance from the top and fasten it securely. Stitch up through the tassel and out at the top. The loose tails of yarn can be used to attach the tassel to your work. Trim the bottom edge of the tassel straight across.

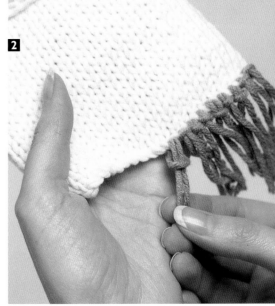

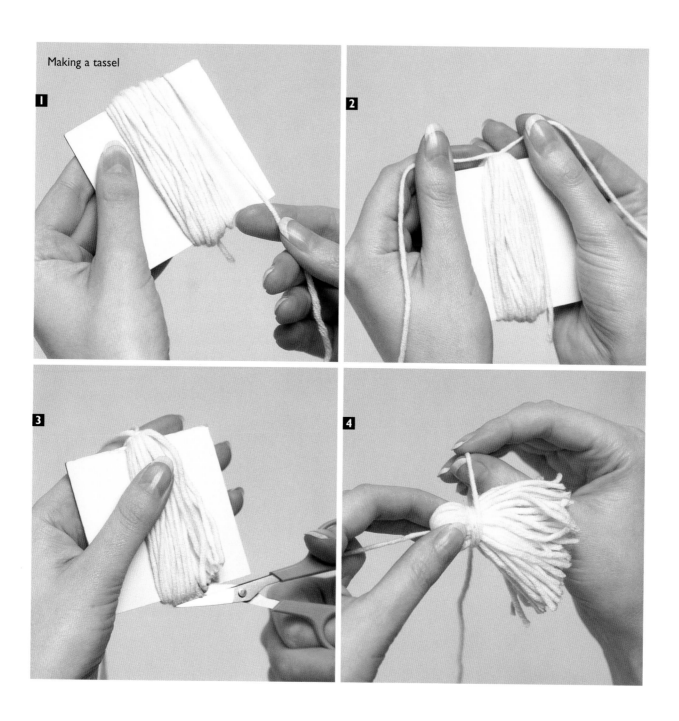

Making a tassel

1

2

3

4

Pom-poms

These decorative balls have a soft, tufty surface created by a whole mass of yarn ends that have been cut to form a thick pile. They can require a surprisingly large amount of yarn to make.

Making a pom-pom

1 Cut 2 doughnut rings of the same size from heavy card. Make the outer diameter of the ring a little larger than the preferred diameter of the pom-pom. The inside diameter should be between a third and a half of the outer diameter; the larger the middle hole, the tighter-packed the pom-pom will be. Place the rings on top of each other and wrap yarn around them until the inside hole is full of yarn. Use several strands at once to speed up the process considerably. As the hole in the centre becomes gradually smaller, you may need to use a needle to get the yarn through.

2 Cut the yarn around the outer edge. Pull the card rings apart and wind a piece of strong yarn around the centre, and then knot it securely.

3 Remove the card rings and trim the pom-pom into shape. The ends of the yarn tying the centre can be used to attach the pom-pom to your work.

Cords

The use of cord has a practical function as a tie or drawstring but it can also be decorative – when stitched around the edges of a cushion, for example. It can be bought ready-made but making your own ensures that the colour matches the piece perfectly. It can be made in many different ways such as with crochet, plaiting and knitting but twisted cord is the easiest and has a very pleasing rope-like appearance. It is created by twisting a number of strands of yarn, then twisting them back on themselves so that they lock together. The more twist, the harder and tighter the cord will be, making it much stronger and more hardwearing.

Making a twisted cord

1 Cut a number of threads half the thickness and about 4 times the required length of the cord. Knot them together at one end and secure to a fixed point, such as a door handle. Take the other end and twist it in a clockwise direction.

2 Keeping hold of the loose end, fold the length in half while keeping it taut so that it cannot tangle.

3 Release the secured end so that the 2 halves automatically twist around each other. Tidy the ends by knotting and trimming them.

Making a pom-pom

Making a twisted cord

Directory of Projects

1 Woven-strip cushion (pp34–5) in Jaeger Matchmaker Merino dk, 100% merino wool. Colours: (A) 783 Charcoal, (B) 782 Flannel. Yarn length: approximately 120m (131yds) per 50g (1¾oz). Finished size: 45cm (18in) square.

2 Superchunky knit throw (pp36–7) in Colinette Point Five, 100% pure wool. Colour: Velvet Damson. Yarn length: approximately 50m (55yds) per 100g (3½oz). Finished size: 100 x 120cm (39½ x 47¼in).

3 Corner-folded cushion (pp40–1) in Wingham Wools Merino Roving, 100% merino wool. Colour: Raspberry Ripple. Yarn length: approximately 70m (76yds) per 100g (3½oz). Finished size: 71cm (28in) square folded to 50cm (20in) square.

4 Chequered cube (pp42–3) in New Lanark Mills Aran, 100% pure wool. Colours: (A) Sandstone, (B) New Natural, (C) Ecru, (D) Sand/Ecru/ Pebble Marl. Yarn length: approximately 162m (176yds) per 100g (3½oz). Finished size: 45 x 45 x 45cm (18 x 18 x 18in).

1

2

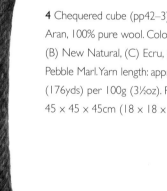

3

4

5

5 Button-edged rib cushion (pp46–7) in Rowan Kid Classic, 70% lambswool, 26% kid mohair, 4% nylon. Colour: 840 Crystal. Yarn length: approximately 140m (153yds) per 50g (1¾oz). Finished size: 45 x 48cm (18 x 19in).

6 Knit-and-purl baby blanket (pp50–1) in Jaeger Baby Merino, 100% merino wool. Colour: 202 Snowdrop. Yarn length: approximately 120m (131yds) per 50g (1¾oz). Finished size: 87 x 73cm (34¼ x 28½in).

6

7 Striped garter-stitch cushion (pp58–9) in Rowan Felted Tweed, 50% merino wool, 25% alpaca, 25% viscose. Colours: (A) 139 Crush, (B) 142 Melody. Yarn length: approximately 175m (191yds) per 50g (1¾oz). Finished size: 26 x 45cm (10¼ x 18in).

8 Striped bath mat (pp62–3) in (A) string and cotton jersey. Colours: (B) ecru and (C) navy. Finished size: 50 x 78cm (20 x 30½in).

8

9 Striped shoulder bag (pp66–7) in Rowan Denim, 100% cotton. Colours: (A) 225 Nashville, (B) 229 Memphis. Yarn length: approximately 93m (101yds) per 50g (1¾oz). Finished size: 21 x 30 x 5cm (8½ x 12 x 2in).

10 Circle stripe cushion (pp68–9) in Rowan Wool Cotton, 50% merino wool, 50% cotton. Colours: (A) 941 Clear, (B) 933 Violet. Yarn length: approximately 113m (123yds) per 50g (1¾oz). Finished size: 45cm (18in) square.

9

10

7

11 Cabled bolster cushion (pp76–7) in Rowan Chunky Cotton Chenille, 100% cotton. Colour: 365 Ecru. Yarn length: approximately 140m (153yds) per 100g (3½oz). Finished size: 88 × 60cm (34½ × 23½in).

11

12 Pillar cable cushion (pp80–83) in Colinette Prism, wool/cotton twist. Colour: 75 Moss. Yarn length: approximately 114m (125yds) per 100g (3½oz). Finished size: 50cm (20in) square.

12

13 Cabled heart hot-water bottle (pp84–5) cover in Orkney Angora St Magnus, 50% angora, 50% lambswool. Colour: 21 Cerise. Yarn length: approximately 350m (384yds) per 100g (3½oz). Finished size: 36 × 22cm (14 × 8½in).

13

14 Contrast-block cushion (pp92–5) in Rowan Kid Classic, 70% lambswool, 26% kid mohair, 4% nylon. Colours: (A) 828 Feather, (B) 816 Wild. Yarn length: approximately 140m (153yds) per 100g (3½oz). Finished size: 50cm (20in) square.

14

15 Fair Isle band cushion (pp100–1) in Jaeger Matchmaker Merino dk, 100% merino wool. Colours: (A) 661 White, (B) 681 Black, Jaeger Extra Fine Merino, 100% extra fine merino wool. Colour: (C) 972 Cocoa. Yarn length: approximately 120m (131yds) per 50g (1¾oz). Finished size: 45cm (18in) square.

16 Leaf cushion (pp104–5) in Rowan Wool Cotton, 50% merino wool, 50% cotton. Colours: (A) 900 Antique, (B) 933 Violet, (C) 929 Dream. Yarn length: approximately 113m (123yds) per 50g (1¾oz). Finished size: 41cm (16in) square.

15

16

17

18

17 Kelim-inspired throw (pp108–9) in Rowan Kid Classic, 70% lambswool, 26% kid mohair; 4% nylon. Colours: (A) 841 Lavender Ice, (B) 828 Feather, (C) 840 Crystal, (D) 822 Glacier. Yarn length: approximately 140m (153yds) per 50g (1¾oz). Finished size: 115cm (45½in) square.

18 Contrast-bobble cushion (pp116–9) in Jaeger Matchmaker Merino dk, 100% merino wool. Colour: (A) 783 Charcoal. Bobbles in Rowan Kidsilk Haze, 70% kid mohair, 30% silk. Colours: (B) 590 Pearl, (C) 604 Caramel Swirl. Yarn length: (A) approximately 120m (131yds) per 50g (1¾oz); (B) and (C) approximately 210m (229yds) per 25g (⅞oz). Finished size: 45cm (18in) square.

19

20

19 Double-wrap-stitch throw (pp122–3) in Rowan Kid Classic, 70% lambswool, 26% kid mohair; 4% nylon. Colours: (A) 832 Peat, (B) 825 Crushed Velvet. Yarn length: approximately 140m (153yds) per 50g (1¾oz). Finished size: 105 × 130cm (41½ × 51in).

20 Honeycomb floor cushion (pp126–7) in Rowan All Seasons Cotton, 60% cotton, 40% acrylic. Colours: (A) 201 Dim, (B) 181 Valour. Yarn length: approximately 90m (97yds) per 50g (1¾oz). Finished size: 45 × 55 × 10cm (18 × 22 × 4in).

21 Ruched throw (pp130–1) in Rowan Rowanspun dk, 100% pure new wool. Colours: (A) 730 Snowball, (B) 739 Icy. Yarn length: approximately 200m (219yds) per 50g (1¾oz). Finished size: 100 × 138cm (39½ × 54½in).

22 Beaded table runner (pp136–7) in Jaeger Silk, 100% pure silk. Colour: 131 Silver Blue. Yarn length: approximately 186m (201yds) per 50g (1¾oz). Finished size: 28 × 141cm (11 × 55½in).

21

22

Knitting Charts

The following charts represent pieces of knitted fabric with each square signifying a single stitch. The symbols in the squares represent the relevant stitch and although most of them are standard, each chart has a separate key. Detailed instructions on how to read the different types of chart are given on pages 48–9 and in the appropriate chapters. You may want to take a photocopy in order to enlarge the chart that you will be working from – you can then keep track of your progress and make notes while you work.

Knit-and-purl baby blanket (page 50–1)

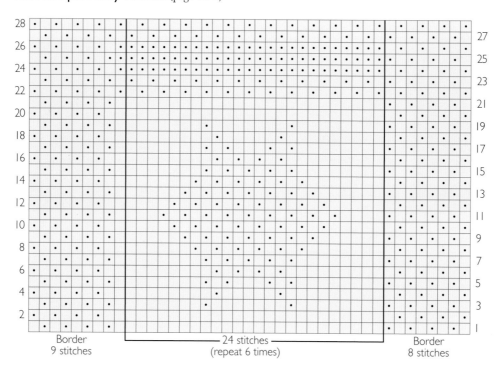

Border
9 stitches

24 stitches
(repeat 6 times)

Border
8 stitches

☐ K on RS, P on WS rows
· P on RS, K on WS rows

Circle stripe cushion (page 68–9)

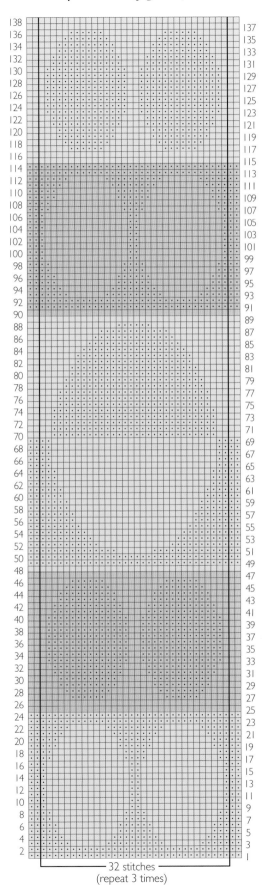

32 stitches
(repeat 3 times)

■ **A** K on RS, P on WS rows
▪ **A** P on RS, K on WS rows
■ **B** K on RS, P on WS rows
▪ **B** P on RS, K on WS rows

Cabled heart hot-water-bottle cover (page 84–5)

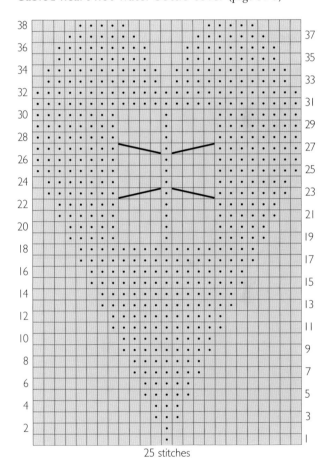

25 stitches

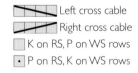 Left cross cable
Right cross cable
■ K on RS, P on WS rows
▪ P on RS, K on WS rows

Fair Isle band cushion (page 100–1)

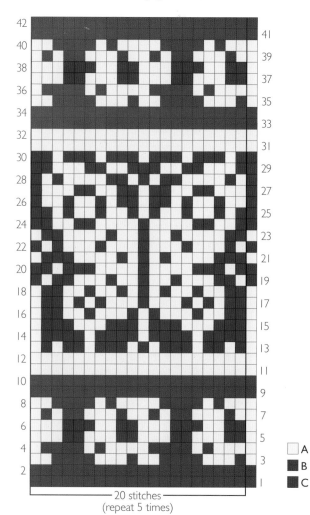

20 stitches
(repeat 5 times)

□ A
■ B
■ C

Leaf cushion (page 104–5)

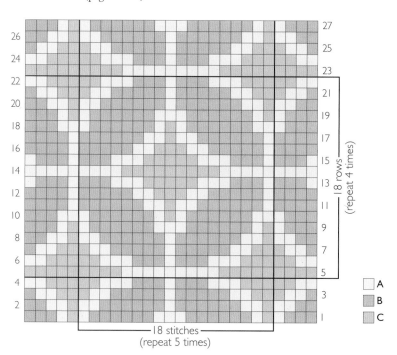

18 rows
(repeat 4 times)

18 stitches
(repeat 5 times)

□ A
■ B
■ C

Kelim-inspired throw (page 108–9)

45 stitches

■ A
□ B
■ C
□ D

Beaded table runner (page 136–7)

Chart 1 (rows 1 to 37)

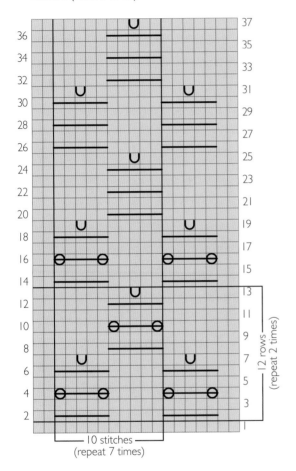

12 rows
(repeat 2 times)

10 stitches
(repeat 7 times)

Chart 2 (rows 38 to 55)

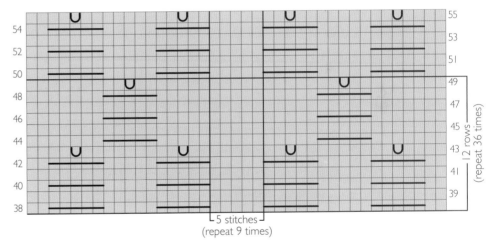

12 rows
(repeat 36 times)

5 stitches
(repeat 9 times)

Strand created by slipping a stitch
with yarn on RS of work

Place bead on strand

Hook needle under strands

Index

Figures in *italics* indicate illustrations.

Suppliers and Acknowledgements

List of suppliers

The Button Queen
19 Marylebone Lane
London W1U 2NF
Tel/Fax: 020 7935 1505
www.thebuttonqueen.co.uk
information@thebuttonqueen.co.uk
A treasure trove of both antique and
modern buttons.

Coats Crafts
Tel: 01325 365457 for stockists.
All the equipment you will need for knitting.

Colinette Yarns
Banwy Workshops
Llanfair Caereinion, Powys
Mid Wales SY21 OSG
Tel: 01938 810128
www.colinette.com
mail@colinette.demon.co.uk
Unique hand-dyed yarns in a multitude of
vibrant colours.

Foam For Home
Freephone: 0800 731 2727
www.foamforhome.co.uk
info@foamforhome.co.uk
High-quality foam, cut to size, delivered
anywhere in the UK.

New Lanark Mills
New Lanark World Heritage Site
South Lanarkshire
Scotland ML11 9DB
Tel: 01555 661345
www.yarnwarehouse.com
yarnsales@yarnwarehouse.com
Spinners of top-quality natural yarn including
Aran in 10 different undyed shades.

Offray
Tel: 01844 258130 or 020 7263 7311
for stockists.
Gorgeous ribbons available nationwide.

Orkney Angora
Isle of Sanday, Orkney
Scotland KW17 2AZ
Tel/Fax: 01857 600421
www.orkneyangora.co.uk
info@orkneyangora.co.uk
More than 30 different colours of
angora/lambswool yarn available, shipped
worldwide with no minimum order.

Rowan and Jaeger
Green Lane Mill
Holmfirth
West Yorkshire HD9 2DX
Tel: 01484 681881
www.knitrowan.com
Comprehensive range of beautiful natural yarns.

Wingham Wools
70 Main Street, Wentworth, Rotherham,
South Yorkshire S62 7TN
Tel: 01226 742926
www.winghamwoolwork.co.uk
wingwool@clara.net
Fibre and yarns for a wide range of textiles.

Author's acknowledgements

Many thanks to the companies listed here (in
particular Rowan and Jaeger), for the beautiful
yarns, buttons and other materials that were
used in the projects. Thank you to my mother,
Pat Birkett, for her advice as well as her practical
help in knitting the projects. Thanks also to
the other friends who helped with the knitting:
Catherine Birkett, Joan Evans and Ros Knight.

Publisher's acknowledgements

The publishers would like to thank the following
people for their contribution: Alma Home,
Baileys Home & Garden, Toast, Smythson,
Emily Readett-Bayley, Tribe rugs, Fandango,
The White Company, RK Alliston, Wallace
Sacks, LSA, John Lewis, Cargo Home, Nicole
Farhi, Pickett, Christie's, Caroline at The Conran
Shop, Vicky and Melanie at House of Fraser,
Gemma at Habitat and Ching at Flax PR.

Recommended reading

Richard Rutt, *A History of Handknitting*,
Batsford 1987.